Ask Beth

You can't ask
your mother

Ask Beth

You can't ask your mother

Elizabeth C. Winship

HOUGHTON MIFFLIN COMPANY BOSTON

Acknowledgments

John Harris, Sunday Editor of the Boston *Globe*, invented "Ask Beth." In 1963 he asked me if I could do such a column, so I sat under a pine tree in Maine, wrote letters to myself and answered them, and felt very wise. When real letters began to arrive, this feeling of wisdom waned. It was then that I discovered how willing and eager are the people who work with teen-agers to share their experience and wisdom. So I am hopelessly indebted to many for their advice.

First and foremost, to Dr. John C. Coolidge, young people's psychiatrist, who has patiently shown me the answers to the thorniest problems, and steadfastly backed my effort to help teen-agers understand themselves.

Pediatricians Ralph E. Ross and John S. Robey advised me about adolescent physical development and problems teen-agers encounter with drugs. Dr. Lester Grinspoon, Associate Clinical Professor of Psychiatry at Harvard Medical School, was kind enough to verify the section on marijuana. Gilbert Marley, who runs The Place, a teen-age center in Concord, had much valuable experience to share. I am especially indebted also to Lawrence McKinney, Director of the Creative Learning Group, for the use of material from his excellent drug education program for schools.

H. William Gregory, pastor of the First Parish Church in Lincoln, helped me directly with advice and indirectly with many a Sunday message. The chapter on schools benefited from the expertise of Terry F. Miskell, who teaches mathematics at Lincoln-Sudbury Regional High School. Dermatologist Dr. Charles S. Keuper contributed essential information from his vast experience with the agony of teen-age acne and other such problems. Mary Glavin, whose sunny presence lights up Richardson's Drugstore in Lincoln, always knows what kids use for this or that, and whether or not it works.

The key to this whole project has been my helpful family. Peggy Cowan, Larry Winship, and Josie Winship, though none of us realized it at the time, provided the fieldwork in how to survive adolescence. Ben Winship, the resident preteen, keeps me on the track right now. My father-in-law, Laurence L. Winship, editor emeritus of the Boston *Globe*, read all the copy and made encouraging noises. My husband, Tom, editor now of this paper, also read, encouraged, and advised, and beyond that liberated his woman with grace and enthusiasm.

Finally, to my editors at Houghton Mifflin, Richard B. McAdoo, who suggested the idea of a book, and Daphne A. Ehrlich, who can cut whole chapters without hurting a bit, thank you very much.

ELIZABETH C. WINSHIP

Lincoln, Massachusetts
December 1971

Foreword

Kids often ask me if I think I can provide any really useful answers to their questions in a column in the newspaper. I tell them that the most useful part of such a column is probably the questions themselves. Everyone is curious about what is happening in other people's lives. It's a bit of human drama. It is interesting, and sometimes helpful, to read what problems other kids are having and see how you are doing by comparison.

All of life is a struggle to get to know yourself better. The struggle is most acute during adolescence. You really don't know who you are some of the time. A fourteen-year-old girl wrote to me: "I have started sprouting and am getting tall like my mother. I thought this would be all there is to it, but I feel I have lost myself. I thought I knew my true self but now I don't really know 'me.' Is this a natural feeling at my age?"

It is a natural feeling. We have all felt this way.

At any age, we may wish to be better, cooler, taller, smarter, happier, richer, or more popular. We look for easy tricks to give us health, wealth, slimness, and bliss. There are many books that try to help. But I don't think there are any very easy ways to get these things. We don't change our basic characters much.

You have to deal with the way you are basically made. No matter how bright you dye your hair, how white you clean your teeth, how short your skirt or frayed your jeans, if you're scared inside that other people aren't going to like you, the mod costume won't do a whale of a lot to make you feel more secure. You need to know why you are scared that other people won't like you. Then you can deal with the real problem.

Finding out who you are helps with all the other problems that may upset you during adolescence. You learn not only how people are supposed to act in a given situation, but how you, the individual, are going to act. The big questions are: How to get along with the other kids; how to be popular; how to get a boy friend or a girl friend; how far to go once you've got one. All these things involve knowing who you are, how you fit in, what you want, what is good for you to have.

Okay, so how do you find out what kind of person you are? You are UNIQUE. But at the same time, you have much in common with other teen-agers' ways of developing and patterns of growth. I keep writing "average" and "normal" and "usual" as if I wanted to lump you all together as "typical teens." I don't. But there are some common patterns that bring common problems to lots of kids between the ages of eleven and nineteen. When you feel perfectly awful, it may be a help to know lots of other kids feel awful about the same thing. Perhaps it won't solve the problem right away, but it can make you hope that it will be solved.

I hope you will find some useful answers to your questions here. I hope you can apply some of the generalities to your individual character, and your individual problem, and find your unique solutions. The girl who wrote this poem is like many of you:

She looks back at Childhood,
She looks forward to Her teens
She thinks of growing up
And She wonders if she likes it,
And She is sometimes lost.
She can't ask Her mother,
Her brother, Her friends.
She has to find herself alone.

Toni Fitzpatrick, Grade 6
P.S. 116, New York, New York*

* From *Young Voices*, collected by Charles E. Schaefer and Kathleen C. Mellor. Bruce Books, 1971.

Contents

xii : Contents

1

What Is Puberty, Anyway?

Dear Beth,
Can you help me? I am thirteen but still undeveloped. I
haven't had my period yet. What is wrong with me? Am I
an irregularity? Will I ever be as normal as everyone else?

Puberty is something you long for. Like the writer of this letter, you hope your sexual development will start at the same
time everybody else's does. But, then you may find it is quite
frightening.

Help! I am very big chested. My mother says I'll get to
my right size, but I'm continuously growing. People tease
me. I hate being the biggest in the bunch.

You expected to be thrilled by your fancy new physical em-
bellishments, but when it is your body filling out, your voice
moving up and down the scale, or your hair suddenly sprouting
in different places, you may be embarrassed instead. But
whether you like these changes or not, you have no control
over what is going on.

At the end of childhood you were probably pretty happy. You were big enough to do most of the things you wanted. You knew who you were. You were in tune with the world.

Now your anatomy is changing so fast your body feels like a stranger's. It is uncomfortable. It sends you different signals, and it doesn't always work well for you. Sometimes you even wish you were a child again.

All this growing up doesn't go by the book, either. Boys are supposed to be bigger and stronger than girls, right? But many freshman girls could eat beans off the heads of the freshman boys. Boys are supposed to be smarter, too, or that was the myth. Are they? No. Many girls find schoolwork easier than boys do in the beginning of adolescence.

There is too much emphasis on the physical things, we all agree, but who can ignore them? Individual differences are so obvious. You can't help measuring yourself against your friends. Some of the saddest letters I get are from kids who have done this, and have come to discouraging conclusions.

Reading about these other kids' problems can be reassuring. It proves that many of them feel the same way you do. It can show you whether your development is in the normal range, or whether it is exceptional, and needs to be checked on by a doctor.

Height

My older brother is tall and handsome. He is a junior and everyone think's he's the greatest. I even do myself, but I am a freshman and I just don't grow at all. He says,

"Cool it. You'll be looking down on me one of these days."
But I don't think I will. Our heights are marked up on
the wall and he was three inches taller at this age.

This boy is impatiently awaiting the beginning of the sudden shooting-up that announces the start of adolescence. It's called, logically enough, the adolescent or prepuberty growth spurt. You grow twice as fast as before. Everything grows — bones, muscles, internal organs — and these changes shape you up for adulthood.

How tall are you going to be? This depends most of all on your heredity. If you come from a tall family, your chances are good of being above average. If your parents are short, you'll probably be rather short too, though there are surprises in both cases.

Other factors affect height. We know environment plays a part, for people all over the world are getting taller. Your parents are taller than theirs were, probably, and your grandparents taller than your great-grandparents. This is especially true in countries like ours where the standard of living is high, and people have had good food and good health for several generations. An impoverished environment, where malnutrition is chronic, can stunt people's growth.

In extreme cases, when a child is growing to be much, much taller than normal, or not growing perceptibly at all, medical treatment can help. The rest of you who are dissatisfied with your height are probably just out of phase with the rest of your friends. Your height, as well as the number of years necessary to reach it, is programmed into your genes. It is all preset. It is the height you are going to be, willy-nilly.

I'm the tallest in my class, and the third tallest in the whole eighth grade. When I'm with my friends, I feel out of place. I know smoking can stop you from growing, but wouldn't it be dangerous to my health? Is there anything I can do besides smoke to stop my growth?

Giraffe

Smoking will not stop your growth, and it is very risky. It is a potential killer. Don't try it.

You are most likely at the end of your rapid period of growth. You can practically count on its slowing down to almost nothing two years after your first period. The average girl grows quickly between the ages of eleven and fourteen and is taller than the average boy of this age. Boys will be shooting past you very rapidly now.

Even if you are destined to be tall, this can be an asset. A tall girl who carries herself well and looks content with her size is very attractive. Tall girls look ungainly only when they scrunch down, trying to make themselves look small. Accept yourself as queen-size.

I'm kind of a big horse. I'm taller than all the boys, and all but two of the girls. Those two are skinny, and I'm built like a Green Bay Packer. I try to be a good sport, but I'm rather clumsy for an athlete, though I'm strong enough. Everyone calls me a "good scout," and the boys seem to like me well enough as a pal. But I don't want to be a "pal." I want to be a girl!

Fullback

A lot of girls who grow early grow not only taller, but also heavier than the others. This extra body size often makes you uncoordinated. Double trouble, but only temporary.

Time helps you learn to handle yourself gracefully. And time makes the boys heavier, so that you are not so big in comparison anymore.

Meanwhile, you don't have to be a tomboy. If you feel girlish, act girlish. Being giggly and coy probably wouldn't be a good style for you, but there is no reason why you can't be feminine and gentle and kind, even though you are a big girl.

And don't undersell the pal relationship. The boys who like you now will like you in a different way as you both mature.

I have a real figure problem. I have been growing a lot lately, but unevenly. My waistline isn't where it ought to be at all; it is way too high. Am I going to be some kind of freak?

Mandy

Nope, you're right on course. Legs quite frequently grow first, which makes your waist unusually high for a while. This is why junior-size clothes come with high waists. You will get reorganized soon.

I am a boy of thirteen, and in the seventh grade. When I was little I was pretty average, but now all my class is growing taller and faster. I'm four foot eight, and most of the boys are already over five feet. Everyone calls me Shorty. Is there any way I can catch up?

Shorty

It is easy to understand why you are discouraged, but many boys don't get going on growing until thirteen or fourteen or even fifteen. You can't push it. You can only grit your teeth, eat well, and wait until your body is good and ready.

However, it can be practically guaranteed that you will add eight to ten inches to your height before very long. This won't make you a giant, but you won't be a midget, either.

I'm a boy of almost seventeen and I'm so afraid I'm never going to grow I can't stand it. Everyone just says, "There, there, you will catch up soon." But I should have started to grow at least two years ago. Do you think I am going to be a midget? Is there anything that can make me start to grow?

Scared

Sixteen is at the upper limit of normal for the adolescent growth spurt, and if you aren't seeing any increase in your rate of growth you may have a hormonal deficiency. See your doctor and find out whether your problem needs to be corrected medically.

Help! I'm growing endlessly. I am already the tallest girl in the whole elementary school. I'm taller than everyone in my family except my father. I have heard there is medical treatment that can stop your growth. Tell me quick before I go through the ceiling.

Alice in Wonderland

Under normal circumstances, nothing is done about limiting a child's growth. Most kids who feel like giants are just ahead of the game. There is help for extreme cases. If a doctor determines that a child is growing to be much taller than the rest of the family, he can give a highly complicated medical treatment that will slow up the growth. However, these cases are extremely rare and the treatment is not a simple one. Most tall kids have to accept their height as a fact of life.

I am embarrassed about my shape. Most of my friends in the eighth grade have much more masculine shapes, and are taller and have bigger shoulders. I still seem to have this baby fat. Kids kid me all the time about my spare tire. I don't eat that much, either. What should I do?

Tub

It's not your fault. Your system just happens to be one of those that takes its sweet time about growing up. Probably your family all matured rather slowly. Exercise and staying off the sweets might help cut down the flab. When your body kicks into high gear and starts growing up fast, your figure will mature by itself.

Girls' sexual development

What's wrong with my body? My girl friends all have boys liking them, but no boy will look at me because I look like a yardstick. Could everyone tell if I wore a padded bra?

What happens to your sex glands is the most important single development in adolescence. This is when you reach the point of no return: you are becoming an adult, and there's no going back to childhood.

The speed with which you mature sexually varies from person to person, just as growing taller does. In fact, those who got tall early are likely to be the ones who mature early, too — though they may not be the kids who especially want this. Kids who do crave to grow up may be shortchanged by nature and stay looking childish while all their classmates sport bras and beards. What inequity!

As with everything else involving sex, the whole process of development is charged with emotion and with secrecy. You often find you can't talk about it to anyone, so your questions seethe around inside like a chemical reaction in a corked bottle. No wonder adults call teen-agers self-centered and explosive.

Naturally it is easier to write to a stranger, so I get thousands of questions from young people who are worried about their bodies. You are anxious if you are ahead — or more anxious if you are behind. You may feel as though centuries are passing while your friends become mature but you stay still. You need to know that 99.9 per cent of *all* teen-agers arrive at maturity in satisfactory condition. Being a little early or a little late is not as crucial as it seems at the moment.

Let's take girls' problems first, since, in most cases, they mature more quickly than boys.

I am going to be twelve very soon, and I am expecting I will get my first period pretty soon. I understand this is normal. I would like to know if there is any warning before a period or any way to know when it is coming. I am afraid I will be embarrassed if I am swimming with friends and suddenly have one.

Worried

You probably will be getting it soon, as the majority of girls (but not all, by a long shot) start to menstruate sometime between eleven and thirteen.

There aren't any definite signs, worse luck. Actually, you don't need them, because a first period doesn't usually begin with a big rush of blood. More likely, you will just notice a few drops on your underpants, or perhaps on the toilet paper. There is ample warning to get prepared, so don't worry about swimming.

Occasionally girls have a little discharge from the vagina before menstruation begins. It is due to other hormonal changes not directly connected with menstruation, and it isn't bloody, but it might indicate that a period is on its way. However, many girls don't have this at all.

I am twelve and a half and have not started any menstruation. I am scared that I am not ever going to because I have always been a tomboy, climbing trees and racing my brothers. Kids say this is the reason I haven't got it yet. Also, I am scared that I will get it, after all, and I don't really know much about it, and I'm afraid to ask. What do I need to know?

Scared Tomboy

You need to know you aren't that late. Most girls have started by the time they have reached fourteen, but some start as late as eighteen.

Being a tomboy wouldn't delay your period one hour. Climbing trees is good for you!

You also need to know that a period isn't really very scary once you have started the process. It sounds frightening, because bleeding usually means there is something wrong. But in this case it isn't so.

What's happening is this: The lining of the uterus gets set to grow a fertilized egg (or ovum). Every month special material is manufactured in there to feed the ovum. If no such egg appears, the material simply washes out, along with some bloody fluid. It takes three to five days for it all to flush out.

Get yourself some sanitary napkins and a belt to hold them up, so you'll be prepared. Ask your mother to pick these up next time she goes shopping, or get them yourself at a drugstore or supermarket. You may feel embarrassed at first, but when you realize that nearly half the population of this country buys them, self-consciousness disappears fast.

Having a period used to be a much bigger deal. Often girls stayed in bed and were treated as if they were ailing. Not anymore. Doctors think it is better for you to lead a perfectly normal life in every way, and that includes swimming and horseback riding.

There can be a few discomforts connected with menstruation, though these aren't nearly as common now as when girls made so much fuss about the whole process. Once in a while a girl gets cramps on the first day or two, or even the day before her period begins. There is a heavy feeling, low down in the abdomen, somewhat similar to being constipated. Exercise may help. Some girls feel mildly depressed, and may weep easily. Most girls have neither problem.

On the whole, having a period is a normal process in a woman's life. So is cleaning your teeth.

I get terrible cramps with my period. Sometimes they even make me sick to my stomach. Unless there is something I just have to do, I usually stay home from school and lie down in a darkened room. But the cramps still don't go away. Is there anything I can take to make me feel better?

Erica

Most girls today have far less trouble than the previous generation. Doctors feel that occasional cramps and depression bother you less if you're active. Those nonprescription pills may help, though doctors try to discourage us from reaching for a pill at every pang.

Severe cramps are unusual. See your doctor to find out what is causing them.

I loathe menstruation! It makes me feel grubby. I actually think I smell, and I am constantly afraid that I will stand up and discover a big stain on the back of my skirt. Help!

H.P.

If you tend to bleed a lot, carry extra pads so you can change them often. Some gals wear two at a time when they are having a flood tide, or a tampon plus a pad. You can also get special moisture-proof underpants for extra insurance.

Sometimes you *do* smell more when you have your friend. Be sure to change sanitary napkins often, and wash more than usual. Be liberal with deodorant. And if you like it, carry perfume in your purse or pocket for a quick antigrub treatment.

I've been menstruating for two years, and never missed a period. Now I have missed two in a row. Is this normal? I started at eleven and I'm thirteen now.

Very Worried

It's not a bit unusual. You have nothing to worry about (I assume you know you're not pregnant), because many young teen-agers are very irregular and sometimes miss a whole summer. If this continues for several months, though, see your doctor.

I have just begun menstruating and I want to know at what age it's okay to start using tampons.

J.B.

The only physical reason some young girls can't use tampons is that there is a layer of thin skin over the opening of the vagina, called the hymen, which blocks the way. With a lot of girls, the opening is only partially covered, so there is no problem. Age doesn't matter. The only way you can tell whether a tampon will work is to try one and see.

Tampons are rather a controversial subject for another reason. Some doctors are afraid that young teen-age girls might get careless (which is certainly possible) and forget they have inserted a tampon. You'd better ask your own physician for advice.

Is there anything a girl can do to herself that can stop her period?

Inconvenient

A traumatic physical experience or emotional stress will sometimes stop the menstrual cycle for a while. However, it is virtually impossible for a woman to do anything reasonable (short of getting pregnant) to stop her period at will. It can be stopped medically.

> *I will be fourteen next month. Last winter my mother bought me a bra, and I was glad at the time. Now I wish I had never gotten the stupid thing. My bust size is 33½ and I am getting bigger every day. My sister is tall and flat chested, and she doesn't even wear a bra. I feel embarrassed in front of my mother, who only wears a 34A. Kids who have been wearing bras two years longer than I have look, and are, smaller. I am ashamed and uncomfortable. I cry every day. My mind is never on my work, and I am constantly looking at myself in the mirror. I don't want to be bigger than a 34.*
>
> *Desperate*

Lots of girls feel ashamed when they first start developing breasts. This may be because breasts are symbols of sex, and you have been raised to be very reticent about sex. It also may be because you have been a child all your life, and suddenly these signs that you are a woman are right there, for everyone to see. Help! You're a little girl. You're not ready for all this yet.

Wearing a bra doesn't make any difference. Breasts are destined to become a certain size, and not even exercises make much difference. Like the shape of your ears or the cut of your nose, your bosom is part of your individuality, and determined by your heredity.

If you feel a lot of shame, talk to someone like your mother or sister about it. You'll feel better. Don't forget you are eventually going to be proud to have a beautiful bustline. I imagine your sister finds her flat chest a dubious blessing.

I am eighteen years old, and practically as flat as a boy. The rest of my figure is normal. Is there something wrong with me? Should I see a doctor? Are silicone treatments expensive and harmful? What about the remedies advertised in magazines? I know beauty is only skin deep, but I'm starting to develop a real inferiority complex about this abnormality. What can be done?

Only Half a Woman

Nothing is wrong with you, and you don't need to see a doctor if the rest of your sexual maturity has proceeded according to schedule. You may develop more of a bosom, but you probably will have to accept being rather small up there.

What is wrong is people's thinking about breasts. The country is abnormal in its passion for large mammary glands. Breasts were invented to feed infants with, and flat-chested women can nurse babies perfectly well. They can have just as good a sex life as their full-breasted sisters, too.

Fortunately, your generation seems to be developing a saner attitude. Current styles don't call for huge bosoms. Many popular fashion models are practically concave. Even movie actresses are now chosen for acting ability rather than chest measurements.

Silicone treatments are expensive, not always successful, and sometimes dangerous. Some doctors feel surgery is preferable to an inferiority complex, but you should consult a specialist about this. I doubt that any doctor would operate until you are at least twenty-one, and have stopped growing.

Those advertised remedies are put-ons.

If you are really upset, buy a padded bra. (But don't wear it too high.) I think they're fine for underendowed eighteen-year-olds — not so hot for twelves trying to look fifteen. Better yet, build up your good points so you don't feel inferior about one shortcoming.

I'll be fourteen in June, and have about a twenty-seven-inch bust. I am skinny. Most of my friends wear bras and my mother says I have to, too, to look grown-up. I don't want to. Do you think I need to wear one in order to get used to it, or should I wait until my bust gets bigger?

Distressed Teen

It takes about five minutes to get used to a bra once you figure out how to get the danged thing hooked up in the back. You don't need to practice. Why not skip it until you feel you will be more comfortable wearing one?

I am twelve years old and very big chested. My mother and sister say I'll get my right size but I am continuously growing.

People tease me about my measurements, which hurts my feelings because I don't like being this big. Sometimes even my friends tell me I'm too big, but I hate being the biggest in the bunch. I can't find dresses and have to wear long bags.

Hurt

Large breasts aren't much use to you at twelve, but the time will come when you won't be a bit unhappy. Big bosoms are desired by most women, so remember that when people tease, they do it because they envy you.

You'll stop developing soon, and the others will start. You will find yourself much more average in shape.

Don't wear bags. It doesn't solve anything to look sloppy as well as big chested. Find loose-fitting but shapely dresses, and hem them.

Is there any harm in going braless? My parents don't approve and my mother checks to see if I'm wearing one every time I go out of the house. My boy friend says, "Go ahead. Be braless." What can I do?

Confused

Parents were brought up in a generation that thought it was sloppy or cheap to wear no bra. They believed a moving bosom was a trick to entice men.

Your mother may also worry that you'll sag. There seems to be some confusion on this point. Doctors say these worries are unfounded, and that in societies where women go braless some fronts sag and some don't, no more and no less than those of their uplifted sisters.

My guess is that bralessness is a fad, and will fade as fast as most fads do. In any case, you are nearly old enough to decide for yourself what is the most comfortable way to dress.

Boys' sexual development

When does a boy know he is a man? When he shaves or when he gets hair under his arms, or what?

Big Red

Most people consider that a boy's first ejaculation is the signal that he has reached manhood. This usually happens three or four months after pubic hair makes its appearance, generally at thirteen or fourteen. It can vary from eleven to nineteen, and those who are late have just as much anguish as "late blooming" girls.

While a boy's primary sex apparatus isn't such a matter of public comment as a girl's bosom, you may *feel* as if it were. Naturally, you want to have equipment of presentable size, but you may have the embarrassing fear that your organ will react without your control. This kind of uncertainty is awfully hard to discuss with anyone.

The arrival of secondary sex characteristics worries you too. It is easier to talk about such things as when your beard will make a showing, or when your voice will get a manly, low pitch, than it is to discuss the changes that are going on inside you. But, on the other hand, these things can be a great source of anxiety to you, because their presence or absence is so noticeable. Perhaps it will defuse some of the shame about these matters to see how other boys are getting along.

I'm not so big as my friends in the masculine way. They rank me down. Will I get any bigger? I'm thirteen and a half years old.

G.W.

You might grow some more. But maybe not. In any case, the important thing is that the myth that a man who is "well hung" is a "super stud" is just that — a myth. All the books on sex (and there seem to be twenty new ones each week) insist that the size of a man's penis has absolutely no bearing on his potency or performance. So if you and your friends are comparing size in the locker room, and they are kidding you for being the loser, tell them they are simply showing their ignorance about sex.

How long is a penis supposed to be?

Wondering

The average length of the erect organ is six inches, but the range is from four and a half to eight. Experts tell you not to worry about your size, but it seems to be hard to stop. Perhaps little boys get an exaggerated idea from looking at their fathers. The adult genitals seem much larger from a young boy's viewpoint. He may have a great deal of concern about his own development because he is trying to match a misconception.

Could you please set me straight on the facts about masturbation? I can't go to my parents about this problem, for fear of what they may say or do. I am a guy fifteen, and I've done it a few times. I hope you can help because I don't even know why I do it.

Uneducated

The first fact about masturbation is that it is practically universal among teen-agers. There is good reason for this. People your age experience strong sexual urges, but there is no socially acceptable way for you to relieve all this tension. And so you masturbate, along with virtually every other adolescent boy. (Plenty of girls do, too, though they seldom write about it.)

Masturbation used to be considered so harmful it was called "abusing yourself." It is now known that it does not stunt your growth, spoil your marks, or ruin your future sex life. Modern research has changed people's thinking about it, and some experts feel it is an inevitable solution to the teen-age predicament. Still a lot of shame lingers on, so no wonder you are afraid to talk to your parents. There is really no reason why you should. You don't have "a problem." The habit almost always fades when teen-agers develop an active social life.

I'm a boy of almost sixteen, and I'm having a hassle with my mother because of wet dreams. She says it is because I masturbate, and it is disgusting, and why don't I stop? Honestly, I don't, unless it's in my sleep. How can I stop doing what I have no recollection of doing?

Misjudged

Your mother's misinformed. Nocturnal emissions are the result of dreams, and dreams are subconscious — you can't possibly control them.

Perhaps your father can enlighten your mother with the straight information about how a male operates. He could tell her that wet dreams happen to all mature males who for some reason, age or otherwise, are not in a position for normal sex activity. Nature relieves the frustration in a dream that produces an ejaculation. It isn't disgusting. He could tell her, while he's at it, that masturbation is no longer considered disgusting either.

I seem to be getting a beard. The fuzz on my face upsets me because the rest of the guys in my class haven't grown any, and they will think I'm an oddball. If I don't shave soon, they will notice the stuff for sure. If I do shave, won't the fuzz just grow back faster? I don't want my friends to think I'm a showoff.

Fuzz Face

Oh, go ahead and shave! If you are destined to be the pace-setter, enjoy it! Though shaving won't make your beard grow faster, it will make the stubble more obvious, but so what? The only kids who razz you will be the boys who are jealous; we always knock others for the thing we envy most. If they think you're faking you can just skip the razor for a couple of days, and your five o'clock shadow will prove your point.

I'm fifteen and my voice hasn't started "breaking" yet. Am I okay?

Bert

You're fine. Lots of voices, about half, change without ever breaking at all. And lots of voices don't change until their owners are over fourteen. Roughly 10 per cent of all boys are sixteen, seventeen, or even older before their manly tenor or bass appears. Don't worry about it.

2

I Wish I Could Be Popular

Dear Beth,

There is this girl in our room I'll call Peggy. She is not pretty, but she hangs around with the older kids so all the boys like her. There are lots of girls in our class who are prettier and have nicer personalities, but the boys don't even notice them. We think it's unfair. Especially when the boys we like say Peggy is pretty right in front of us. How can we be popular like Peggy?

We all want to be popular like this girl, all of our lives. Kindergartners like to have lots of friends. Fourth graders want to be elected president of their class. Adults need to be liked, too. But concern about popularity is at an all-time high during the teen-age years.

One reason you care so much about how you rate with other kids is that you are just getting out from under your parents' wings. Your family used to give you all the love and support you needed. Now you have to turn to your friends for it. So you don't just *want* them to like you; it's crucial.

Another reason adolescents are worrying about popularity

is obvious: the opposite sex has suddenly raised its interesting head. Somewhere along about junior high school, you want this very specific kind of popularity. It ought to be easy. The boys want the girls to like them. The girls want the boys to like them back. What stands in their way?

The two biggest problems are shyness and lack of social technique. You feel awkward, insecure, and inexperienced. So how about those kids who seem to attract others to them like flies to a honey jar? What is the secret of their success? Are they better looking than other kids? Not necessarily. Natural beauty has its advantages, sure, but many popular kids are quite plain. Is it their clothes? Their intelligence? Their wit? Not necessarily, though any of these can help. What these kids have is charm. They seem to feel more at ease socially, so other people feel good when they are around. They have some self-assurance; they are outgoing and friendly. They can talk to other kids. They can care about others, too.

There are books that try to give you techniques for being popular. They say that if you pick up the right tricks, you can be the most sought-after kid in your class next week. Unfortunately, it's not that easy. First you have to figure out how you feel about yourself. You have to like yourself in order to be able to like other people. If you don't have the inner confidence that you are a likable person, the techniques won't do you any good.

Poise *can* be learned once you have some confidence. Teaching yourself to be attractive to others is one of your most important jobs right now. You can learn how to dress becomingly, and to talk easily so you can converse with friends and strangers. Above all, you need to learn what your good qualities are —

and everyone has some — so you can present yourself to the world as a person worth knowing.

> *I have only one close friend that I can really talk to. Oh, I know a few other girls fairly well, but I wouldn't say I was one of the most popular girls in my class. Do you think this is okay, or should I try to make more friends?*
>
> *Lone Ranger*

Most kids have only one, or maybe two, really intimate friends. It is important to have somebody you can tell your inmost feelings to, but it isn't necessary to broadcast them all over the countryside. What is definitely not okay is to have no close friend at all. I'd say you are doing just about right.

> *I'm a sort of average guy, and there's this boy in our class who I find myself hating. He is really well built and a natural athlete, and every time we are picking people to do anything, he'll be the first one chosen. I'm getting so I can't stand the sight of him. I guess I'm jealous. Should I try to get more popular, or just forget him, or what?*
>
> *P.B.*

It's natural to envy these lucky few who seem to swing through life and have everyone tripping over themselves to be their friend with no effort on their part at all. But they are the exceptions.

How popular do you think the average kid needs to be? He needs to be accepted by his classmates as a good person, valued for his own particular personality. He doesn't have to be in competition with the rest of the kids to see who is going to get the most friends.

Stop pitting yourself against the class hero. If he's a nice guy, admire him. It doesn't lessen your image at all.

I'm shy

All teen-agers feel shy in certain situations, at certain times, or with certain people. You have never been this grown-up before. You don't know how to talk or act or look in the new world you're in. Your chassis has been redesigned, but the motor is racing, the brakes grab, the wheels are out of alignment, and the timing is erratic. If you can't trust the machinery, how can you feel secure?

So okay, it is normal to feel shy, and you'll get over it. You will grow accustomed to yourself and your surroundings, you'll observe others, and though it takes years — six or seven or eight — by the time you're twenty-one or so, you will have developed confidence and poise.

But suppose you are one of those many teen-agers who feels really stymied by your shyness. What makes you so worried that you stammer, blush, or perhaps don't even dare talk at all? Fear. The basis of shyness is the exaggerated fear that you won't measure up to the rest of the kids. You're convinced that they think you aren't any good, so you want to hide.

When you find out what you are really afraid of, you will see that it isn't true. You *are* as good as they are. Nobody is expected to be perfect. You have to stop worrying about some vague inadequacy that doesn't exist. Until you do, you will be afraid to let other kids get close for fear they will discover that you aren't a "good person." You'll be afraid to speak up in class lest you reveal that you are bad or babyish. And these fears are groundless. Not realistic at all.

Shyness with the opposite sex goes back to childhood, too. The natural curiosity little kids feel about sex is unacceptable to adults. Words like "dirty," "disgusting," and "shameful" fly through the air. Children get the mistaken idea that *they* are somehow dirty or shameful. Then when they are in their teens, and expected to have some sexual feeling, it still makes them feel ashamed and shy.

What can you do about it? Everyone has some feelings of shyness, but kids who have poise know how to avoid situations where they might feel ashamed. This is something you can learn. As you slowly figure out that most of your fears are unrealistic, you begin to master your shame. You realize you're just as good or bad as everyone else. You don't have to reach impossible standards. You feel you fit in; you begin to like yourself. Then others can like you, too.

People always say that bold and brassy girls don't appeal to boys, but they are wrong. The most popular girl in our grade is really bold. She goes up to any boy and puts her arms around him. She talks with everybody, even teachers, in a flip way. All the boys really go for her.

I dream of being as easy with kids as she is, but I know it will never happen. I'm almost sixteen, and I'm very shy. I don't think any boy will ever like me.

Invisible

Sure some boy will like you. This girl is getting along well because she takes all the social initiative. Everyone can just sit back and let her do the talking and hugging. It's easy. So they like it — at first. Real brassiness gets pretty boring after a while, though. This bold girl may not be very popular at all in a year or two.

You are shy because you somehow believe you aren't as good as other people. Though this fear is grossly exaggerated, still you believe it, and think you will be shamed if you stick your neck out. This feeling makes you run away from social situations.

Shy people all exaggerate their inadequacies. You will eventually realize this. Already, half of you wants to be sociable. Talk to girl friends and teachers. Stop thinking of others as enemies. Right now, you are your own worst enemy. When you succeed with these relationships, you will start feeling more secure. You will begin to develop the confidence you need to go still further — and even talk to *BOYS*.

I'm having awful trouble in high school with girls. I come from a family of all boys, and I just can't get used to girls. When I'm around them, I sweat and stammer and blush like a jerk. I feel as if I can't look at them. How can I get over this? I don't want to spend my life running away.

Jerk

Does it reassure you to know that most boys feel this way? Not all are as painfully shy as you are, but most are distinctly uncomfortable around girls at some point.

Experience is the only cure. Just being around girls every day in school will make it easier for you. You are attracted to girls. That's good. You're supposed to be, even though it makes you feel shy now. It may take a year or so before you find a particular girl you feel you can communicate with, but it will happen. As soon as you give a hint that you can be approached, girls will notice it.

It doesn't matter if you are always a little shy. Some girls like a little shyness in a boy. So hang in there.

My boy friend is shy. I try to bring him out, but I don't know if he really likes this or not. Sometimes he seems to, but other times he doesn't. What am I doing wrong?
Encourager

Try to figure out what you were doing when it seemed to make him feel good. Was it different from the things that made him clam up? Were you too obvious? Did you embarrass him in front of others? Work on what you were doing right, and it should up your average.

Ever since I can remember, people have been telling me that I'm pretty. I have been so conceited about my good looks that everyone is starting to hate me. How can I get rid of my conceit?

Narcissa

Conceit is usually a cover-up for another feeling — fear. Some people like you are convinced that they are no good, or actually ugly or dirty inside, so they put up a big bold front, of superiority. They hope others will fall for the "I'm so great" image, and not suspect what they secretly fear, that they are really not great at all.

You have a sort of reverse shyness. If you had real self-assurance, you wouldn't bother to compare yourself to other people. You would be content with the way you are. And you really are okay — not awful at all. Try to accept your real self. When you can start liking yourself, you'll be able to let others like you. You will stop being so concerned about yourself all the time, and develop a warmth and understanding that will draw kids to you — your old friends, and new ones, too.

I am a loner. I don't have many friends, either boys or girls. My family says I am self-centered. How can I counteract this and have more social life?

Kenneth

As a teen-ager, you *have* to be concerned about yourself. You have to find out what you are really like, and what kind of an adult you are becoming. You are turned inward trying to sort out thoughts and feelings.

Most teen-agers feel insecure about reaching out to others. They are afraid they will appear foolish, or different. Their hands and feet feel too big. They're afraid they will do something awkward or clumsy.

Your parents should try to understand how much of your interest has to be centered on yourself just now. This is not a character fault. It is the way you grow up. It would be more useful if they tried to help you grow more comfortable with your new adolescent self.

You can work at this, too. You will be less concerned with yourself as age and experience give you confidence. Stop hiding what you feel from others. Share your feelings with them. Respond to theirs.

Share your interests. Do things with other people. Tell them what interests you, and find out what they care about.

Be generous, not just with money, but with your time, your praise, and your friendliness.

Trust your own friendly feelings. When you find out that they work — that others like you back — this discovery will be the best antidote to your doubts and lonesomeness.

With it or not

I'm twelve years old, and my mother won't let me wear nylons. Everybody *else my age is wearing them. Don't you think she's being unfair?*

This is a cry from the past. Nobody has asked me about nylons for the last four years. But kids still concern themselves about how they look. Do you know anyone who can walk by a mirror without sneaking a peak?

Everyone wants to look right, to conform to the group, with just enough difference to be a little bit individual. How different do you want to be? Just different enough so you still feel safe. Some teen-agers like to dress "way out." Others prefer to be indistinguishable from their friends.

Style itself varies so with place and time that the only way to know what's being worn is to open your eyes. If your style of clothes, your hair, and even your face are (1) right, (2) becoming, and (3) comfortable, then you can forget how you look. That's the ideal condition.

My two best friends used to be tomboys like me, but now all they want to do is talk about clothes, and how to fix their hair. Sometimes they will play what I want to play,

*but other times they say I'm babyish. I'm twelve, and I try
to get interested in clothes, but I find them boring. Should
I be?*

Blue Jean

Well, you will be pretty soon. What you wear is one of the
first things people notice about you. If you want to make a
good first impression, it matters to you what you have on. When
you get to be a teen, you will care a lot how you impress the
opposite sex. That's when you, too, may start to care about
clothes.

*I have a pair of white flared-leg pants, low hipsters. I'm
not fat, but a little on the hippy side. I think these pants
look good on me, and one of my friends does, too. The
other says I look like a cow in them. How do I know who's
right? How do you tell what is really becoming to you,
anyway?*

Sara Ann

Consulting friends is usually a good way to find out. Especially friends who have a good sense of style. Another good
thing to consult is one of those three-way mirrors in a dressing
room. You can't hide much from that clear rear view it gives
of you.

*This girl in school is a real kooky dresser. When we
were all wearing mini skirts, she wore knee lengths. Now
we wear long dresses, and she is wearing culottes. And it
doesn't seem to matter at all. I wore a midi skirt I made,*

and everyone laughed and made fun of me. How come she can get away with it and I can't?

Wondering

Either this girl is totally unconscious of her appearance — just couldn't care less what others think — or else she is ultra-conscious, and so sure of herself she can be a pacesetter.

Those who are in between like you, like most girls, in fact, feel uneasy if their clothes are very different from the norm. So they can't carry it off with aplomb.

There's a girl in school who dresses as if she were going to sing in a nightclub. She wears passionate purple eye shadow and false eyelashes two feet long. Now that low necks are in style, she wears hers down to where you can practically see what she had for breakfast. We think she looks cheap, but the boys don't. They are all over her like a tent. It makes us mad! Should we copy her sexy clothes, or what?

The Plain Janes

Don't copy her. It wouldn't come naturally to you. And anyway, her attraction for the boys won't last. The classic seductive female looks like a real sexpot, and the boys cluster around, but they soon find out she isn't so sexy after all. In fact, the chances are she doesn't even like boys very much, but is a "scalp collector" who wants a string of conquests. She probably isn't capable of loving very much, and is going to be a sad person later on.

When the boys find out there isn't much genuine feeling behind the exciting exterior, they'll come drifting back to you plain (perhaps) but warm and pleasant Janes.

I have my heart set on one of those bathing suits that has cutouts in the front and back. My mother put her foot down. She says it's "immodest." Honestly, it doesn't expose half as much as some of the bikinis my friends wear. Don't you think it would be okay?

Beachie

I know what you mean. A lot of bikinis aren't much more than two hankies and a shoelace. But there is something to be said for modesty, just the same. If you show practically everything you have, it doesn't leave much to the imagination. And it's the imagination that keeps boys interested. Don't you want to keep boys interested?

How do you learn how to put on make-up so it's right? I haven't started to wear it yet, but I want to know for when the time comes.

Interested

Lots of girls visit the cosmetic counter of a good department store. The beauty consultant there will analyze your face and show you how to use various products to help create a good effect. Different shades of foundation, for instance, can seem to change the shape of your face or your nose or your chin. Eye make-up can accent eyes, minimize a big nose. There are thousands of tricks.

She'll want to sell you some of her cosmetics, and you'll probably want to buy some. Then practice at home. And consult friends and teen-age magazines. It's clever to test it all out at home before you appear in public. If you have to wear make-up, a good rule is to wear just enough to cover up your defects and accent your good points.

Most of the girls where I live are wearing some make-up, but I don't feel like doing it. I wear my hair long and my face plain. My friends call me a square. Will I be out of things if I don't use any lipstick or stuff?

J.P.

There is always a problem when you go against your crowd. In this case, though, I think the tide is running your way. The "natural look," which means using no artificial devices of any kind, such as curlers and face paint or even girdles and bras, is growing. Look at this year's Sears Roebuck catalogue, and you'll see that the models have no obvious make-up at all. This style will be popular for some time, I believe, as it ties in with the current trend to be concerned about ecology and conservation. Sound far-fetched? Well, conservation concerns man's treatment of the earth versus nature's, so leaving your face the way nature made it does have some connection.

Yesterday I spent hours getting ready for a dance. I washed my hair and set it in a new way that my girl friend said was becoming. I did my nails and scrubbed my face, and I had a new dress that is so pretty. My dad said I looked stunning. Even my brother said I looked nice! And guess what? I got to the dance and nobody danced with me. Not once! I cried all night. Tell me, what did I do wrong?

Miserable

It is important to look nice. Very. But many teens make the mistake of thinking it is the *whole* key to popularity. They blame their failures on wrong clothes or fat legs or a big nose. Well, looks help at first glance, but after that it is your personality and how you come across to other people that keeps you going.

If you spend hours getting perfectly turned out, and then go to a dance and plunk yourself down, expecting miracles to happen, they don't. You have to put more effort into *being* nice, not just looking nice.

The personality myth

Your personality is the visible aspect of your character — how you strike other people. It has to do with how you look, which we have just been talking about, and how you talk, which we are going to talk about next.

The myth is that you assume a new personality, just like a new suit, if the one you have doesn't seem to be working well for you. There is lots of advice about this, from "How to Win Friends and Influence People" to "They Laughed When I Sat Down at the Piano." These are tricks you can use. You can learn to play an instrument or remember people's names, and it might help. Basically, the thing you want to do is not change, but utilize the stuff you already have . . . Play up your attributes, and soft-pedal the weaknesses.

But before you know yourself very well, you may not be sure what these attributes are. So you may try too hard in one direction or another. Or fake it. Here are some kids' experiences.

Everyone says that if you want to get ahead, you have to have a "good personality." How can I have a good personality when I don't even know what my personality is? I'm not sure it has developed yet.

Steve

You are born with a personality. Each person has qualities and abilities and talents in various combinations that make him different from everyone else. And your life has already shaped these to quite an extent. A teen-ager's major research project is to find out what these are in his particular case.

You analyze your friends a lot. You know what qualities you admire in them. You can turn the same process on yourself, and decide which of your own qualities to develop as the most likable, and which ones to squelch as undesirable.

Adolescence is a time for testing. Try new situations, contacts, and activities. Discard the experiences that don't work out for you. Eventually you will develop a sort of tally sheet, so you can say, "Steve is a guy who is good company, but not very funny. Enthusiastic, not original. A good sport, but not competitive. Can dance, can't sing. A good mathematician, lousy at languages." And so on. Then you'll begin to understand more where you fit in, and where you're going.

I'm attracted to a girl in my English class. She's a really classy blonde, and damn good-looking. She seems to like me a little, but I never get anyplace with her. She doesn't go for anyone else, either, as far as I know. She's a book freak, though, and I'm not too much of an English student. Should I read up on poetry and try to get her interest that way?

No Student

That depends on whether you are no student because you haven't tried, or because you have no talent for English. You can't change your personality to one that you have no basic tendencies toward. A pseudointellectual gets defrocked very fast. However, if you've just been lazy, go ahead and give books a try. You might even get hooked, and that's a plus even if you don't get the girl.

Making conversation

The boy sitting next to you stares straight ahead in mute agony. You search frantically for something to say to him, but each idea sounds sappier than the one before. How do you start talking to someone you just met?

This is one place where there are tricks you can learn that really do help. And knowing the tricks helps give you nerve enough to try.

Most people enjoy talking, once they get over that beginning hump.

Boys seem to find it even more difficult than girls. My stack of letters that open with "What do girls like to talk about, anyway?" is about three times as high as the pile beginning "What do I say to a boy?"

So if you're one of the millions of kids who find this sort of thing tough, collect a few good openings to have ready when needed. Once you have got a question or two out into the air, the other fellow will probably give you some help. Probably. But even if you hit a conversational dummy, the fact you have made some kind of an effort will make starts two and three so much easier.

When I'm introduced to strangers, or when I meet new people at parties, I never can think of anything to say. How the heck do you begin a conversation with somebody you have never met before? You don't even know what kind of question to ask them or what they like.

Stumble Mouth

Make small talk. Find out who they are and what they are interested in. Ask where they come from, where they go to school, what they like or dislike most in school, what sports or hobbies they have.

You aren't trying to start a deep discussion about Marcuse or civil disobedience. You are trying (a) to keep both your mouths going so you aren't just standing there going "duuuuuh" with a frozen grin on your face, and (b) to find out a little bit about this person.

What do you do when you're stuck with this dude at a party and you have asked all the right questions, and it turns out the guy is only interested in cars, cars, cars? I don't know anything about cars except how to open the door. How do you talk about something when you don't know beans about it?

Moira

Use your head! Suppose you really did want to know something about cars. You'd keep asking questions until you found out what you wanted to know. This is a good technique.

Many teen-agers (probably more boys than girls) not only can't start conversations well but also have trouble keeping them going. If you can draw them out by leading the talk into their area of interest, and then field them enough questions to

keep them throwing back information, you are successfully pro-
moting conversation. A boy will like talking about his interests.
You will like having got him talking.

A tip. Part of the success depends on *how* you ask as well as
what. Your interest must come across as real. You must listen
to his answers, so you can develop more questions from them.

One-sided, yes, but hopefully just at the beginning. If he is
a nice guy he'll want to listen to you after a while. If he's not,
you don't want to be his friend.

*You are always telling girls how to meet boys, but you
never tell boys much about getting on with girls. Everyone
just assumes that boys know what to do, but I don't. I'm
not nervous, but when I see girls I know nearby I don't
know what to say. What subjects interest girls?*

Helpless

When you were in elementary school, it was no problem
talking to these girls. Can you remember what you talked about
then? School, teachers, other kids.

Girls are still interested in these things. It's easier talking to
girls you know, because you are familiar with the same things.

Ask a question. How did you like the beans at lunch? What
did you think of the French test? Wasn't it freezing in gym?

It doesn't hurt to think up a few subjects to talk about ahead
of time. Then when a girl suddenly appears, you are armed
with a "Hi. How did you make out with the math homework
last night?"

*What is all this jazz you give about people liking to talk
about school and teachers and their hobbies and stuff? You*

know what people really like to talk about — themselves!
Just listen to what people around you are saying sometime
and all you hear is "I think . . . ," "Well, I feel . . . ,"
"I believe that . . ." The problem isn't to start conversa-
tions — it's to stop people from telling you a whole lot of
stuff about themselves that you don't want to hear.

Sick of "I"s

I was dealing with beginning conversations with people you don't know well. It is better not to try to get too personal when you have just met someone for the first time. If you started out with "Do you sleep on your back or your stomach?" or "What kind of deodorant do you use?" they'd think you were moving in too fast.

You have a point, though, that's valid. It is never a good idea to overload your conversation with too much about yourself. Leave half, at least, for the other guy.

I'm a junior in school and I don't have any hang-ups
about talking to people. I don't get embarrassed around
girls or anything like that, but I have this thing about ar-
guments, and it is getting me down. When people start
getting all excited and yelling at each other, it bothers me
so much I just want to split.

When kids ask me what I think, I don't seem to have any-
thing to say. I know it sounds dumb, but I really don't
know what I do think about Vietnam and politics. My fa-
ther and mother never talk about politics. Can you help?

Sam

People who aren't used to hearing arguments confuse them with fights. Of course, people can get very hot expressing different points of view, but it isn't the same as being mad at each other for personal reasons.

I expect your parents hate arguing. You will have to learn to accept arguments because you will hear them all your life. Some people *love* to argue.

It can be helpful to know when to change the subject.

I also suggest you read your paper and the news magazines and do some selective watching on TV. Then you will begin to develop your opinions, and you'll find yourself eager to express them — and defend them.

> *Why am I so loud? I cannot, no matter how hard I try, moderate my actions or my voice.*
>
> *Recently a boy told me, "You just want to be the center of attention." I answered, "Yes, you're right." But why? I'm fifteen and I wish I could shut my big mouth!*
>
> *A.K.*

Everybody wants to be popular, and at your age you are more concerned with your public image than at any other time in your life. Something inside you keeps impelling you to get yourself noticed — with the idea that this brings popularity. You are new at all this; you get excited and go overboard.

Now that you notice you are going too far, you can see the attention you are getting isn't all approval. Realizing this means that you can check yourself. Practice talking quietly — perhaps at home, where you feel more confident. Practice waiting before you jump into action. If you get this habit, you will learn in time to stop being loud before you start.

Flirting

I work in a laundry after school, and there is a boy who comes in regularly. He only brings his own clothes. (His mother comes in another day.) I like him and I think he likes me. How can I get to know him better?

A.T.

Flirt.

*

Once you have screwed up courage to talk with the opposite sex, you don't need any pointers on how to flirt. When you really like another person, you may feel giddy and silly and begin making eyes. And why not? It's natural. Look at all the things animals do to attract the attention of a mate. The penguin, for example, lays a stone at his beloved's feet.

Don't bring stones. But go ahead and be gay. Life without gaiety is as bland as a boiled egg without salt.

My girl friend is mad at me. She says I'm a flirt, and I'm not. We met a couple of guys at the hamburger joint we always go to after school. We liked them a lot. I was talking to one of them, and teasing him because he was eating so much. He didn't seem to mind. In fact, I think he is going to ask me out because he wanted to know what I do on weekends. But my friend says I was flirting. Was I?

Margo

Yes, and what's wrong with that? Flirting is only a way of teasing that lets a guy know you think he is attractive.

You tease, usually by exaggerating something about the boy.

"Man, you sure eat like a bird!" "How can a little shrimp like you [assuming he's a hulk] put away all that grub?"

This kind of talk is banter — light, good-natured teasing that you know will get his attention without hurting his feelings. You flatter. You kid. You smile while you do it, and maybe glance at him out of the corner of your eye, or even flutter your eyelashes. Doing this is instinctive with a lot of girls, and it can be very appealing if you can do it without looking too coy.

I like a boy named Dave. We have known each other for years at school, and have talked together quite a bit. I like this.

I want him to take me out, but he seems shy about asking me. One day I decided to really play up to him, so I sat close and tried to look into his eyes, and well, you know. He didn't do much, but he didn't ask me out. Now I think he is even colder to me than he was before. Did I blow my chances with him?

Wants Dave

You may have. Boys, especially shy ones, really get nervous if girls come on too strong. Passionate looks, heavy breathing, and other actions that mimic the seductive stars of the silent screen scare boys because they suggest too much too soon.

Boys like Dave don't know how to handle it, so they retreat back into their shell.

Your clue is to keep it light and easy. Most teen-age boys don't like girls who are too aggressive, especially in a sexy way. Darn few grown men can cope with a really seductive female very gracefully either. A man likes to take the initiative himself. Girls can hint — which is flirting — but they shouldn't come on like gangbusters.

3

Problems of Face and Figure

Dear Beth,

I've got so many problems I don't know where to start. My hair is so thin it's pathetic, and to make matters worse, it's bright orange. I can never tan, so my complexion is a mess. And I'm too thin so my shoulder blades stick out. The kids who don't call me "Orange Pop" call me "Chicken Wings." I hate the way I look.

Looks matter. A lot of people think kids don't care how they look anymore. They see a bunch of high school students sitting on the lawn in front of school, and because their hair looks long and clothes look freaky to adult eyes, they conclude that students are no longer concerned with their appearance. They are coming to the wrong conclusions.

Parents who see the care that goes into picking the long skirt or the fit of the frayed jeans know this. Parents who hear the anguished cries as another pimple pops out just before a special date know their kids are deeply concerned with their faces and figures.

There can be such a contrast between the way you'd like to look and what you actually see in the mirror! You hope to see a tall, slender, smooth-skinned creature with an intelligent look and cool gaze. Instead, you confront a lumpy, pimple-faced, irregular, three-quarter-grown individual with a shifty, scared, or disappointed expression.

This discrepancy doesn't help the self-image. And this is just the time when some confidence in how you look to the outside world would be so great; Lord knows you feel shaky enough inside as it is. The last thing you need is overproductive sebaceous glands, unequal body growth, plugged pores, glasses, braces, and all the other woes of adolescence. But that's what you're apt to get, and there are two things you need to remember all the time:

(1) It's temporary. Ninety-nine per cent of teen-agers outgrow these defects.

(2) It can be helped. What modern medical knowledge can't cure, today's beauty chemistry can probably disguise.

And above all, learn to live with what you are. Do the best you can with your outside — then forget about it.

Complexion complexes

One high school girl described herself as "a nice package done up in lousy wrapping paper." The epidermis does take a terrible beating during adolescence. Acne is a scourge to many, and it doesn't play fair. You can keep as fit as a Derby winner and still have pimples. It used to be thought that what you ate did the damage. Many teen-agers do have voracious appetites for French fries and chocolate milk shakes, but doctors now are pretty certain that diet is not a major cause of acne. Some kids are sensitive to certain foods, and these foods may hurt their complexions. Avoiding fatty foods such as pork, nuts, and chocolate, as well as fried foods, is a good idea for everyone.

Getting upset, or emotionally excited, can trigger the sympathetic nervous system to act up, and this in turn will get your oil glands to overproduce. This is why your face sometimes betrays you just before a really big date. What a system! Some kids have glands that just seem more prone to producing acne. More boys than girls get acne. Some girls get it before they have their periods. These things are beyond your control.

What you can control is keeping your skin clean, and exposed to light and air. One aspect of today's youth culture is counterproductive from the point of view of good complexions, and that is a casual attitude toward cleanliness. Bacteria do not promote a clear skin. So kids who feel that dirt is part of nature might make an exception to hands and face until they are past the peak acne period.

Other ideas many kids have today are going to benefit them. Eating health food — if the diet is properly balanced — is fine for the skin. So are hiking and bicycling and all forms of outdoor exercise.

Getting a golden tan is another matter of interest to teenagers. So are freckles. But acne is the biggest problem, and there is one message that holds out hope for all. Almost all acne clears up before adulthood. And almost all acne clears up without leaving scars.

Is it normal for a person under twelve to have more than occasional pimples? Does it mean anything? I mean, does it mean I will have acne when I'm older?

Very Worried

It probably means that you are maturing a little faster than your friends. It is normal to have some pimples during adolescence. The oil glands in your skin start producing more oil at this time. For some reason it doesn't all drain out through the pores very efficiently. Some pores get clogged, causing blackheads. When these get infected, you get a pimple. Most kids have some.

Doctors don't really know why some kids get acne and some don't. Having a few pimples doesn't mean that you will — or that you won't. In any case, keep your face scrupulously clean, which will help keep the condition from worsening. Massage your skin gently with warm water twice a day for five minutes; it will help unclog the pores. If you also use an antibacterial soap, it will check the infection that is causing the pimples. When you want to go out, cover the spots with a medicated cosmetic.

Some people were alarmed by recent findings that hexachlorophene caused brain damage in mice. Authorities feel that the use of this chemical in soap, which is applied only to a small area, and then rinsed off, is perfectly safe for adolescents. The FDA has not removed such soaps from the market. However, if you're nervous, use a soap containing sulfur. Or any good soap, for that matter.

I am fifteen and have blackheads all over my face. Should I squeeze them out, or what? I'll do anything that will help me to banish and discontinue these spots!

Polka Dots

Don't squeeze. The blackheads are clogged pores; oil is trapped in there, and mixed with dirt, which makes it black.

You might squeeze it in, instead of out, and you'll probably force germs into the pore and cause an infection. Either result may leave you with pimples, or worse, and possibly a scar. Hands off is the best advice for all skin troubles.

See your doctor. He may remove the blackheads with a special instrument. He can certainly tell you the best way to eliminate these blemishes. This will undoubtedly involve lots of warm water and perhaps a special soap.

I've had a terrible case of acne, and I've done everything they told me, but I still get these horrendous pimples, and some of them are leaving pits. Help!

Ken

It's a temptation to say you probably haven't kept your skin as clean as you should have, or that you have been inadvertently picking at the blemishes, which is almost unavoidable in bad cases. But who cares whose fault it is? You need professional help. You are getting secondary infections, and had better get to a doctor fast. He may give you antibiotics to clear up these abscesses, or change your diet.

I wash my face three times a day, but after a week of washing, my face is so chapped it turns red. What should I do?

P.F.

Lay off the soap for a while. The massage and warm water are the most helpful, anyway. When the chap is gone use soap sparingly.

My complexion is terrible. My father thinks it is because of sex, and this is so unfair. I don't know any boy well

enough even if I wanted to. Which I don't. My mother be-
lieves me, but my father is being awful to me.

Abused

Your father is 100 per cent wrong. So are all the people who
think that *lack* of sex causes acne. The matter is purely local —
too much oil in the pores.

I have far too many freckles, and don't know how to get
rid of them. With summer coming on, they'll just get
worse. Is there anything I can use or do to make them dis-
appear?

Spatter Puss

No way. Those lotions that claim to lighten brown spots
don't do anything. You're right about sun accentuating freckles,
but is it worth it to stay inside all the time? Buy a big hat and
daub the spots with the best sun lotion.

Lots of people find freckles attractive — on others. They
think freckles give you a pert, outdoorsy look. If you don't share
this view, hide them behind make-up.

Tanning your hide

I like to have a nice golden tan, so I sun-bathe a lot, but
someone told me this is bad for your skin. Is it? And how
come cowboys and sailors can be out all the time?

A little sun goes a long way. That way is toward dry,
wrinkled, and prematurely aging skin. Also, premalignant

spots may develop. These are not so malignant as other forms of cancer, but cancer just the same.

Cowboys and sailors are moving around. The harmful rays have a more direct shot at you when you lie still. But men who work outdoors a lot do get cancerous growths, too. Watch those rays.

How do you tell which product to use to prevent sunburn? There are about a zillion kinds in our drugstore, and they all claim to give you this gorgeous, even tan. Well, I'm very fair, and all I get is a gorgeous all-over burn. Help!

Lobster

The Food and Drug Administration says: "There is nothing that will prevent sunburn except staying out of the sun."

New formulas are being worked out which will have sunscreening ingredients that filter out 80 per cent of the solar rays. The stuff you can buy right now offers adequate protection for an hour, at least. However, swimming and sweating reduce the effectiveness of sun lotions.

Look for lotion that advertises itself as "preventing sunburn," for under federal law, these products must list their active ingredients. The chemicals you want are: para-aminobenzoic acid; isoamyl p-N; N-dimethylaminobenzoate, compound salicylate, or benzophenone.

Slather yourself every hour, oftener if you swim. Wear a hat, and start sunning *slowly,* only five or ten minutes a day, until you have a protective tan.

Once you wrote about some pills you can take to help tan white spots on skin that never get brown. What are they called? Are they expensive? Do you need a doctor's prescription?

Ammo

They are called Trisoralen, and are rather expensive, and you do need a prescription. They help the cells in these white spots manufacture the pigment that produces a tan. They work well if you follow directions faithfully. See a dermatologist.

I'd like to use a sun lamp, but I've heard it causes cancer.

Bilious

Doctors don't feel that sun lamps are a direct cause of cancer, but overexposure causes the same skin problems as too much sun, and can make skin prone to cancer. It is safe to use them in moderation. A correct dose is one that gives your skin a nice pink glow. A deep, bronzed effect, which may look great today, will hasten the aging of your skin. And who wants sags and wrinkles any sooner than necessary?

Shapes and sizes

No two figures are the same, but the flaw that causes the most problems is fatness. Overweight kids write more often than underweight kids by about 100 to 1. Perhaps the slim ones know they are doctors' pets for health and longevity. But I doubt it. They just know it's stylish to be skinny, and the Twiggies aren't complaining. (Except the girls would like to wear a B-cup bra.)

Why are so many of you too fat? Doctors now think it is

mainly because you were raised to be fat. Family eating habits are one reason. Diets that are heavy on the bread, gravy, and doughnuts produce kids that are heavy on the scales. Lots of well-meaning mothers get the mistaken idea that a fat baby is a healthy baby. Love that rising weight chart? Stuff that howling mouth!

We have a national tendency to reward goodness with food. If junior doesn't cry at the dentist's, we give him a lollipop.

There is the compulsive eater, whose problem is caused by emotional hang-ups, but most of us are just conditioned by habit to race to the cookie jar in times of stress or strain. We aren't rotund, but we tend to be chubby.

Whatever the reason for it, if you have too much flab, you have got to take charge of reshaping yourself. Your mother can help, but the will power has to come from you.

It's impossible for me to lose weight. I've tried every diet there is, and sometimes I lose a little, but then I get off on an eating jag again and pile it right back on. Lots of my friends say they have had good luck with a high protein diet, but I've failed so often I'm afraid to try again. Do you think it would work for me?

Lois

There is only one formula for losing weight — eating fewer calories than your body burns up in its daily activity.

Crash diets, starving yourself, skipping meals, eating just cottage cheese and grapefruit, and even the high protein diet have no magic except that they cut down on calories. The problem with most of them is that you are starved for some kind of food, and apt to go back for what you have skipped with a vengeance.

The high protein diet *can* work, for a time anyway. Its advantage is that you lose quickly, which gives you encouragement to go on, and you drink so much water you don't feel very hungry. Its disadvantage — and don't ignore this — is that it is not a well-balanced diet. Good nutrition matters more when you're still growing. Omitting certain foods can do you permanent harm. Talk to a doctor before you try it.

I'm FAT! All my high school friends are dating, but I know I haven't got a chance because I'm such an ugly tub. I pretend I don't care, but I do. I've tried a hundred diets, but don't have the will power to stick to any of them. I'm scared all the time about what people will say. There must be some help for me. What can I do?

Big Slob

To get help sticking to a diet, you might try the Weight Watchers. It's a commercial organization, so it costs a little money, but the important thing is that you get the moral support of other dieters having the same problems you do.

For $2.50 a week you go to a meeting where you're weighed, you hear a lecture about losing weight, and you can discuss your own case with experts.

This group gives you a good diet, which you must follow strictly. But it's liberal, so you don't feel starved. The group's main objective is to re-educate you to eat sensibly the rest of your life.

Don't hate yourself for being fat. You got that way by mistake. Try to reshape yourself. I'm sure you can do it.

I'm in love — with chocolate. I gave it up for a week and I was miserable. All the kids in my room eat chocolate

*as if it's going out of style. I need not to. How can I stop,
or cut down?*

Chocolate Chub

To stop eating one thing, start eating something else. Stock
up on stuff that is okay for you — fruit, carrots, sugarless gum,
or diet candy. When the craving for chocolate begins, stuff
your mouth with these.

If you can find a friend who also needs not to eat rich goodies,
get her to join you. Sit away from the chocolate stuffers and
eat celery, and think about what awful tummies the other girls
will get.

*I'm sick of girls who can only brag about how skinny
they are, and bore our ears with monotonous droning
about diets, and how they just "eat like a bird." Most of
them are nervous wrecks.*

*I like a girl who is cheerful and has interests in life other
than her stomach, even if she is well endowed in that area.
How about a plug for the plump?*

Norman

You've got a point. Dr. Hilde Bruch, a specialist on obesity,
says this about overdieting girls: "They are unaware of how
much their tension, bad disposition, irritability and inability
to pursue an educational or professional goal is the result of
malnutrition."

The popularity of skinniness came about through the medical discovery that obesity is unhealthy, and the TV discovery
that thick middles look even thicker on the screen.

Staying slim is great, but carrying it to the point of malnutrition and monomania is ridiculous.

I am a fourteen-year-old boy. I'm skinny and unmuscular. My physique is so bad that I'm afraid to take off my shirt when I go swimming. How can I gain?

Garret

First of all, see your doctor. You may be a "late bloomer," and time will pack on muscle for you, or you may be not eating enough, or not eating well. He can tell you what your ideal weight is for your height and bone structure. Some people are just designed to be leaner than others. He can also recommend a good diet.

Here are some tips for gaining:

If you can't stuff three times a day, eat six small meals.

Ask your mother to cook "fat" — to give you foods with more calories.

Eat a bedtime snack. An eggnog or malted, with a cheese or a peanut butter and jelly sandwich, will stick to your ribs.

Get plenty of rest. Try adding an extra hour in bed each night.

Get plenty of exercise, too. This is just as important for twigs as for tubs. The way to the good physique is to make muscle, not lard. Outdoor exercise is particularly helpful because it perks the appetite.

Finally, when you reach a good weight, readjust your eating habits so you don't go too far in the other direction.

I'm much too big on top. Other girls tell me I'm lucky, but I can't see why. All the guys keep whistling at me, and

*the styles nowadays are meant for sticks. How can I make
myself look smaller?*

Pouter Pigeon

Have you tried the bras that are designed to make big breasts
appear smaller? Several companies make them. Shop around
until you find one that does most (or least) for you.

Don't make the mistake of trying to hide under a tent dress;
you'll just look big all over. You need a waistline, but a natural
one, not a high or Empire waist.

Tight sweaters are no good. Raglan sleeves and dresses or
blouses that are cut with a curved seam at the sides de-emphasize
big fronts.

Pick your dress fabrics carefully. Clinging, loose-woven, or
fuzzy stuff is out. Crisp, tightly knit material in dark or sub-
dued colors minimizes size. Jazzy patterns above the waist won't
help, but if you wear gay skirts or pants with quiet shirts, attention will be deflected from top to bottom, which you want.

Avoid horizontal stripes like poison ivy. Vertical ones are
excellent. So are up-and-down braid trims, rows of buttons,
and any other details that accent the straight-up line.

*I'm a fifteen-year-old boy who has an extra-large rear
end. I'm so self-conscious I rarely tuck in my shirts. I can't
lose weight, because I'm skinny everywhere else.*

Big Bottom

If it's fat you've got back there, you can reduce it with exercise. Swimming or jogging will help a lot. So will specific
floor exercises. Lie on your back, arms outstretched to either
side. With knees straight, bring your feet up to your right hand.

Now, keeping shoulders flat on the floor, raise both legs straight up and swing them over to touch your left hand. Then sweep legs down in a big circle, brushing the floor, and up to your right hand again. Repeat the exercise several times, then change directions. Work up to eight each way, twice a day.

While still there on the floor, raise your hips as high as you can, then bang down on the floor, spanking yourself as hard as your older brother would spank you on your birthday.

If your rear is solid muscle, you can't make it go away. You probably can stand up straighter, so it doesn't protrude. Flatten yourself against a wall until your hand can't get in between your back and the wall. Try to walk around maintaining this position several times a day.

A couple of my girl friends and I have abnormally muscular legs. We'd like to get some fat off our thighs, but the only way is through diet and exercise, and the exercise would give us more muscle. Any suggestions?

Muscle Bound

Swim. Lots of people mistakenly believe that if they exercise, their fat will simply turn to muscle, and they'll be worse off than before. 'Tain't so. If you went on an Olympic training schedule, and ran four hours a day, you might get outsized muscles, but mild regular exercise plus sensible diet trims off fat without enlarging muscles unattractively.

Swimming is particularly good for redistributing weight. Dancing would do it, and would also be lots of fun. Same with biking. Remember, though, that some legs are not built to be pipestems, so just do the best you can and then quit worrying.

My mother keeps after me about my posture. I know I am sort of hunched over, and I don't want to get round shouldered, but how can I remember to stand up straight?
Robin

You're probably hunched over because you are feeling insecure about the world. Lots of teen-agers do this. When you regain your self-confidence, and feel physically, emotionally, and mentally on top of things, you'll stand up straight, as a matter of course.

Some people have crooked spines, and need medical treatment, but by and large, good posture is a matter of feeling good, all over.

Hair! Hair! Hair!

It's a thorn in the side of parents, and a matter of great importance to kids. If it weren't, the musical that broke records in so many theaters wouldn't have been called by this name.

What's the trouble with your hair? Everything! You haven't got enough. You've got too much. It's too long, too short, the wrong kind, the wrong color. You want it on your head, not on your legs. It won't grow on your chin, if you're a boy. If you're a girl, it *will* grow on your upper lip.

Hair is definitely one of the first things you notice about people. In some cases now, it's almost all there is to see. Naturally you want it to behave the way you'd like. Perhaps there is some help for you here.

I have to wash my hair every other night. My parents say I'm washing all the oil out of it, and it will be bone dry by the time I'm twenty. I'm sixteen. Is it bad to wash it so often?

Shamp Champ

Not if it's really oily. It is better to wash out the grease, which collects a lot of dirt, than it is to let your hair stay dirty.

Frequent washing does stimulate the oil glands. Instead of being bone dry at twenty, you're more likely to be good and greasy. But even so, it's better to shampoo. And the oil production may slack off as you reach maturity.

My hair is now about two inches below my shoulders. I'd like to have it really long before the summer, but it grows very slowly. Is there anything I can use to make it grow faster?

Lazy Hair

Nope. Can you afford a fall?

I'm disgusted with my hair. After I wash it and it is dry, it's very straight and looks nice. But when I wake up in the morning, it's all wavy again in the back. What can I do to prevent this?

D.G.

Tape it down flat in the back before you go to bed. Make sure to use nonsticky professional hairdresser's tape. If your hair is long, wrap it tightly around your head.

My hair is terribly dry. I never wash it, practically, and it still is dry and impossible to do anything with.

Pat

Do wash it. Also brush with a really good natural-bristle brush. A lot. You need to activate the oil glands, and anything that massages your scalp will do the job. You can also use a shampoo for dry hair, and ask a barber or hairdresser about conditioning lotions.

I have a lot of dandruff. Mother says it's because I don't rinse my hair enough, but I've stayed under the shower until I was as wrinkled as a prune, and still the snow keeps falling.

Herb

A little snow is just the natural dead skin flaking off. A big itchy snowstorm indicates infectious dandruff. Sitting under Niagara Falls won't cure that, but there's some stuff that will—a shampoo that is a detergent suspension of selenium sulfide (Selsun). You need a doctor's prescription. It doesn't smell like Bay Rum, but it works, if properly used.

I have some dark hair on my face and upper lip. It's not too noticeable but it bothers me. What can I do about it that a college girl's budget will allow?

Catherine

There are several options, and not knowing just how thick your budget is, I'll list them in order of ascending price, which means (wouldn't you know?) ascending efficiency as well:

Shaving. Costs practically nothing. Lasts one or two days. Leaves unpleasant-feeling stubble, but does not stimulate growth any more than other methods, despite common theory that it does. However, five o'clock shadow is a threat.

Bleaching. Costs little. Lasts a month or two. Makes hair less noticeable, but only less.

Depilatory cream. Costs a little over a dollar. Removes hair for about three to five days. No stubble problem.

Waxing. Costs a fraction more. Lasts for several weeks. Hurts on the tender part of the face, unless you have it done in a beauty parlor. Then it calls for a fat budget.

Electrolysis. Costs around five dollars a treatment. You might need two or three treatments at the start. Then a repeat every few years. Feels like weak mosquitoes biting you. Far and away the most permanent solution.

I have some black hairs on my stomach which look terrible in a bikini. Can I remove them with wax?

Hairy

If you have a Spartan streak. Otherwise, try a less painful method such as depilatory cream.

I tried to grow a mustache last summer, but it came out thin and straggly. My friends all kidded me. I still want to grow one. Is there anything I can use?

Clark

Use patience. Neither expensive lotions nor greasy kid stuff can fertilize a mustache. Facial hair does get thicker as you get older. In a couple of years you may be able to grow bushy enough to shame a walrus.

But some men never have very much facial hair. Be prepared to forget the project, in that case.

B.O. and bad breath

I take a shower every morning with special soap and load on the deodorant, but by lunchtime the effect has all worn off. My clothes turn yellow under the arms. Kids make fun of me, so I try to avoid them.

B.O.

Teen-age glands often overproduce — sweat glands included. Nervous stress and strain make you sweat all the more. So B.O. can be a big problem, and it comes as quite a shock because before you are eleven or twelve you usually don't smell.

There is plenty of help. First you have to wash with an antibacterial soap to get rid of the little stinkers that cause the odor. If you have trouble during the days, take soap to school and wash again at noon. Then there are antiperspirants to check the wetness, and deodorants to disguise the aroma. They are not the same thing. You can use both if you have to.

Some kids feel that this country has gone crazy trying to wash off, spray, and deodorize every vestige of human smell. They say we are trying to turn ourselves into synthetic, antiseptic products, and they want no part of it. I can sympathize with this idea, but one trouble with it is that we aren't nature's creatures anymore. We live in heated houses and wear clothes and this makes us different from bears and lions. When we sweat, the stuff stays on us until we wash it off.

So even if you are a nature freak, you can use unscented

soap. You can also use dress shields. These are good for the yellow-armpits problem.

Is there any way to deodorize after swimming? I hate going to the bathhouse to spray on deodorant each time I go swimming.

B.A.N.

Unless you have an unusual problem, you needn't spray more than once. Most deodorants don't wash off in water. You have to lather them off with soap. If you swim for hours and hours, or sweat like a horse, it might be a good idea to tuck a purse-size sprayer in your beach bag. But don't worry excessively. You are all out of doors, and a small whiff of human perspiration isn't going to make the boys flee in disgust.

I hate to ask a girl to slow-dance because my hands sweat so much. Boy, do I need help. I wash my hands frequently but it doesn't do any good.

Errol

You sweat because you're nervous. You'll get over it when you feel at home dancing. Spray your hands with antiperspirant — not a deodorant. For extra insurance, carry a handkerchief to mop your palms.

I love this boy very much, but he has halitosis. And when I say halitosis, I mean HALITOSIS. It's hard to be in the same room with him, let alone dance. We can't just be friends outdoors. How can I tip him off without ending our relationship?

Gassed Out

Carry peppermints and lifesavers, and keep offering them to him. There are also some excellent sprays now on the market. If he questions this, tell him he *needs* them. If he doesn't get the point, I think you could come right out with it, tactfully. He shouldn't feel hurt, because you are showing that you like him.

When your body lets you down

Some of the difficulties that face you during adolescence are temporary. Clumsiness, braces, face or body out of proportion — all are connected to the way you are growing up. When you've finished growing, they will have corrected themselves, for the most part.

Other problems you have may be with you forever. No one is ever completely satisfied with the way he or she looks. Noses are too big, ears stick out, and legs are too heavy. How much these things get you down is largely up to you. We all know really funny-looking people who are happy, outgoing, and loved by all. They aren't emotional cripples. And we all know people who are so self-conscious over some figure fault — heavy legs, pointed ears, or something — that they spoil life for themselves and people around them. Suppose you are ugly or have a handicap . . . How do you learn to live with it?

I'm a pretty good athlete, but in other ways I'm clumsy as a bear with five legs. I can ski and skate. I'm even on the varsity basketball team, and I never have any trouble during games. But then, on my way home, I'll probably trip over the curb, or walk into the house and smack into the sofa. I'm always dropping things. What's wrong with me?

Two Left Feet

Your body just hasn't adjusted to all the physical changes adolescence has brought to it. It can't function perfectly while some parts are out of phase with the rest, and the machine isn't synchronized. You aren't used to your size.

Nervousness makes it worse.

When you are playing a game, you have no trouble, because you are concentrating hard, and gross motor movement is what's needed. At other times, your mind is on the inner turmoil that concerns all teen-agers, and it's not watching out for sofas and curbs. Fine coordination — the kind you need for carrying things — isn't your forte at the moment. The more you hate yourself for looking clumsy, the tenser you get, and the more you fumble.

Be of hope. So long as you play varsity basketball, there is nothing physically wrong with you that time won't take care of.

I have to wear braces. I think I'm ugly with them. I wish I could get a boy friend, but I know nobody will like me while I have all this wire in my mouth. How can a boy kiss a girl who wears braces?

Tinsel Teeth

May I give some advice to Tinsel Teeth? Don't develop a complex about your mouth. Two years ago I was condemned to wear braces. At the time, I was going with a boy and I learned a lot about kissing . . . Boys want other qualities in a girl besides hot lips.

Don't be afraid to smile. You don't have to grin from ear to ear, but please don't keep a straight face for two or three years. Play up your good points. Play down your mouth. No lipstick.

Literally thousands of girls have braces. If immature kids throw wisecracks, the way to live through it is out-laugh them. When the dentist pulls off those wires, you'll have beautiful teeth and a better kind of personality to go with them. Good luck.

One Who Lived Through It

I have just found out that I have to get glasses. I think it is a disaster! Don't boys hate girls who wear glasses?

Prilly

With all the glasses you see today — from little-old-schoolteacher specs to great big bug eyes, boys must either love 'em, or they'll have to stop liking girls.

Pick out a really becoming type of frame, even if this means trying on every pair in the store. Then go home and sleep on it before you make your choice. Glasses can be an asset. You can also learn to take them off at just the right moment.

I'm well liked by all my friends in school, and I have a fairly good figure. But I have an awful face! When I'm introduced to people I feel they are thinking how ugly I am. My mother won't let me wear make-up because I am only thirteen. What can I do?

Ugly

You may not be too happy with the way you look now, but this isn't the way you are going to look later. Thirteen-year-old faces are incomplete. Parts have grown up and parts haven't. It makes them out of proportion.

While you wait for your mature face to appear, think a bit about appearances. Do you only like beautiful people? Or are you attracted to smiles and expressions that tell you this person is interested and wants to like you? When you are introduced, try to communicate friendliness. It will help you stop worrying about what they may be (but more than likely are not) thinking about your face.

I am a boy with a really misshapen nose. My parents have finally agreed to let me get a "nose job" if it doesn't cost too much. Does it? Do I need a specialist? How long is the hospital stay?

Moose

It costs from two hundred to five hundred dollars. This doesn't include the hospital stay, which is from two to five days. You definitely need a specialist, and what he would do is remove some cartilage, sometimes some bone, too, from the nasal septum.

Another thing — this operation, called "cosmetic surgery," is not usually covered by health insurance.

I have enormous ears. Kids say I look like a car with both doors left open. I am really getting a complex about this. Is there an operation to whittle them down to size?

Dumbo

There is an operation to make them stick closer to your head. Many surgeons believe it is well worth a bit of surgery to keep kids from the misery of self-consciousness if their problems can be easily corrected.

However, there is a chance your ears will turn out to be the right size when you are fully grown. Consult your doctor.

I was in an automobile accident, and one of my legs was badly smashed. I'm still on crutches, and it may never be quite right. One of the things I can do is swim. I want to go to the beach with the gang this summer, but my mother says absolutely not. Not because it would be dangerous, either, but because she says my scars will look terrible in a bathing suit, and I shouldn't impose them on my friends.

I wear mini skirts and hot pants, and no one seems to mind. Is she right?

N.J.

No.

Everything is to be gained by your living as normal a life as possible. It's so great that you want to go swimming, and shows you have made a fine adjustment.

You have learned what your mother needs to learn, that when there is something "different" about you, a game leg or birthmark or whatever, other people take their cues from you. If you are relaxed, friends get used to it and are not embarrassed. Of course, strangers may take a second glance, but who cares? It would be a shame if your mother allows her discomfort to interfere with your wonderful unself-consciousness.

Why don't you ask her to visit you at school and see how unconcerned your friends are? I think it will make her proud to see you facing the world with such good cheer. And I hope this will change her mind about the beach.

I have an ugly face. I'm a junior, so I know it isn't just "part of growing up." The nose is long, the eyes too close together, and the chin is practically nil! The last two years have been rugged. I have learned to ignore the wise remarks, and I get along all right because I have a lot of good friends, although I don't exactly enjoy being called "Pig Eyes" or "Chinless Wonder." My question for you is not what should I do about this, as I know all I can do is put up with it. I want to know what makes kids so unkind. Sometimes really good guys say things that make me squirm. How come?

No Romeo

Kids are usually unkind because they are unable to see another person's point of view all the time. Teen-agers are learning how to love and they can be the kindest and most understanding friends much of the time. Then they can turn right around and be thoroughly heartless. They haven't enough maturity yet for sustained compassion. They can't always rise above their own feelings to save another person from hurt. The truth is that not many adults are capable of unfailing kindness, either. But most grownups have learned to be tactful, and to control their hurtful impulses.

This explains why kids are *thoughtless* sometimes. Deliberate cruelty is something else. It is caused most often by the tremendous importance of "image" to teen-agers. Status means more during high school years than any other time, and the easiest way to make yourself look big is to make the other guy look small. This image-building affects even the nicest guys. They make cracks about you when they have suffered some confidence failure of their own, and need to polish their image in their friends' eyes. The scapegoat is usually the person who has some strike against him already. You. And others.

When your friends grow more secure, and confident of their roles in society, their need to pick on other people will lessen. I wish I could say disappear, but finding a scapegoat is a basic weakness that some adults, some groups, and even some nations continue to indulge.

You show tremendous wisdom in your response to your problem. If you can keep up this mature attitude, I feel sure you will find that the worst is already over. You will reap such benefits in human relationships that eyes, noses, and chins will fade into irrelevancy.

*

Perfection of face and form is a matter of taste. Different places and different times admire different things. In Nigeria, they put young girls in a "fattening room" and stuff them until they weigh three hundred pounds. This is what Nigerian bridegrooms have been taught to want. It shows them their bride's family had enough wealth to feed her.

I don't know how many Nigerian girls make three hundred. I do know no one is perfect, even by our standards. That classmate who seems so serenely unchallenged by any blemish probably has flat feet and a nervous stomach and would like to be two inches taller. Serenity means he or she isn't letting this interfere with happiness.

There is no point in yearning for the unattainable. You'll never make it. Maturity is learning to live with what you were dealt by nature. And then putting your energy into more interesting phases of life.

4

School

Dear Beth,
I'm getting so I hate school. I can hardly drag my body
to the bus every morning. I used to get A's, but now I just
don't seem to care anymore. I make resolutions to do all
my homework, but then I break them. I really like one of
my teachers, but he's mad at me and so is everyone else.
What's wrong?

This is a very typical letter. I never hear from a teen-ager who says, "I think my school is neat and my teachers are all nice, and so are my friends. Is anything wrong with me?" It's the school haters who write, which gives this chapter a negative tone, with some justification.

School is pretty much your whole life in adolescence. It's your social arena. It is where you try to find out who you want to be and where you match yourself against others to see how you're coming along. Finally, it's where you *have* to be. You have no choice, which lends a note of desperation to your situation sometimes.

Teachers report an all-time low of academic performance

in junior high school years. Puberty doesn't exactly put a person in a serene, untroubled state of mind for concentrating on the books. Kids also become more critical of adults at this time. You care more about what your friends think than what adults think. You don't want to do nice, neat work anymore just to please teacher. You aren't sure the system is so great. And then there's the opposite sex. How can you think about math when someone you like very much is peeking at you over their shoulder from the next desk?

So you find work hard and boring. School stinks. Sometimes the problem is inside you. Sometimes the problem is with the school. Men like John Holt, Jonathan Kozol, Paul Goodman, and James Herndon have exposed some bleak places in our conventional public school system. Reform is in the air, but there are miles to go before there is uniform high quality.

You have to evaluate your situation with all the objectivity you can muster. If you are having a learning problem, get some help. Discuss it with your parents. Perhaps you can change schools. If you're stuck in a bad school, try to salvage your self-esteem and get what good you can from these years. Usually there is a chance to do something to improve your predicament.

I absolutely despise my school. The teachers are always after you for something. I'm always in trouble for talking and fooling because I'm bored silly with school. I "lack attention and cooperation," they say. It's true I seldom do all my homework. There is only one teacher I can stand well enough to ask when I don't understand things.

I can't quit school; I'm only in the eighth grade! I also can't quit because I like the kids. I'm sure you will say this is natural for someone my age, but my case is really serious.

Bored Stiff

Alas, it is natural. You have written a classic description of eighth grade woes.

It isn't so much that you talk and fool because you are bored. Something inside you compels you to this kind of action. And you are bored because you talk and fool. It is truly hard for many young teen-agers to pay enough attention in class to keep interested. Quitting or transferring wouldn't help. You have to outgrow this whatever school you are in, city or suburban, parochial or public.

Don't give up trying to learn to control yourself. Do throw yourself into whatever does interest you, as it will use up your restless energy, fend off depressions, and give you self-respect to succeed at something. Talk to that teacher you like. He or she can probably give you some personal advice that will help you do adequate work both for your sake and to meet the school's standards.

We are sophomores in high school and feel that we are wasting 90 per cent of our time here. The stuff we have to study, like geometry and French, has no relevance to real life. We ought to be doing more with current events and ecology and things like that.

Also, we don't have enough extracurricular things except band and chorus. There's a drama club, but the teacher who heads it is bad news and no one wants to be in it.

Our school dances are boring and the student council doesn't do anything. No one in our group has any use for this school.

Moira

Relevance is a hard thing to judge. What seems relevant to you now may not be when you are older. You have to rely somewhat on adults to know what is likely to be relevant in an adult world, but only somewhat. Kids who have discovered the relevance of pollution and racial imbalance and things like that have injected blasts of fresh air into some school curricula.

These were kids who acted. Your group seems to have the idea it is fashionable just to be bored. Do something about your grievances. Run for student council and pep it up. Form a student committee and ask the faculty to add the material you want. Get on the dance committee and put some life into it. Schools usually help students who show that positive changes can be made.

Our school is pathetic. It's a big, brick jail and it's crowded and the halls stink. The teachers act like policemen more than like teachers and yell and scream orders. The principal is a nothing; the janitor has more authority than he does. I'm not kidding. When you do something wrong, the teachers say, "I'll send you to the janitor."

I know you'll say it's my fault and I ought to try harder, but I don't think it's true. Funnily enough, I like to read and do it a lot at home. You can't read in this school. It's too noisy. I'm failing in two subjects.

I have read some books about schools like Up the Down Staircase *and* The Way It Spozed to Be, *and I think this school is just as bad. What can I do? I feel grungy all the time.*

May

It sounds as if school is failing you rather than the other way around. Teachers and parents are sometimes quick to blame kids for having a "poor attitude" or "not working up to their potential." Perhaps both things are true, but only because bad teaching is making the student "lazy" and "inattentive."

If your school is boring and inadequate, it is vital for you to realize that this is not your fault. Many of you who try but don't learn, who want to pay attention in class but can't concentrate, who would like to be interested in their subjects but find nothing to arouse their curiosity take all the blame on yourselves. You may squawk loudly and say the school stinks, but deep down you feel it is yourself who is the failure. You go through your days lugging a burden of disrespect for your own abilities which is not warranted.

It is hard not to blame yourself when adults say it's your fault. Adults are supposed to be right. There must be something to what they say. This is what is making you feel grungy all the time.

If your school is bad, it's bad. Some schools unfortunately are. If the teachers yell, the halls smell, and the principal has abrogated his responsibilities to the janitor, it is no good for people to tell you this isn't so. You can see it. To deny it implies your judgment and standards are faulty. One *ought* to disapprove of a badly run institution.

To survive, you have to stop feeling that the responsibility for the bad scene is your own. Somehow you have to keep your own integrity and self-respect in spite of it.

What can you do? You have to stay at this school, and daily life will be easier if you go along with the rules. Some kids can't. They rebel and fight back. This makes their lot thorny, though it is hard to condemn them for rejecting what they find a hopeless state of affairs. Perhaps you are so disgusted that you have overlooked some positive things. In such a large place there should be an interesting teacher or two, one course that is better than another, some good kids. Grab any good experience you can.

Can your parents stir up some community interest in improving the school? Can you get outside help in failing subjects? It is no fun to fall back.

Try to find nonschool projects you can value. Help out in the library, or get into music, or get a part-time job — anything available that can build your self-regard by letting you do something you like, and do it well.

Exams, homework, and marks

Exams loom like Mount Everest to many students. Adults don't get judged like this very much. Nobody gives Mother a C for dishwashing. The income tax doesn't get sent back marked "This is too messy. Do over." Grownups face tests, but not like these, and they should have compassion for the downright fear you feel in the face of exams.

Homework is the subject of many other wails of complaint. There's too much of it. Your parents bug you too much.

And as for marks, they are probably the biggest single worry about school. One thing that is too bad is the constant comparison of one kid's marks with another's. They don't mean the same thing. Your C in history may indicate you have worked hard, done the best you could, and achieved quite a bit of knowledge. Jane's C may mean she hasn't cracked a book, has kissed off her homework, but crammed for the exam, and did well. She will have forgotten most of it by Thursday. Perhaps marks will be abolished someday. Meantime, keep them in perspective. They show how you progress. They aren't little goodies to collect for themselves.

And whenever you have trouble, feel unfairly treated, or can't understand, do try appealing to your teacher for help. Most teachers are pleased when a student cares enough to ask. You'll find it's much easier, too, to learn on a one-to-one basis. You don't have to compete with classmates. You don't have to be embarrassed at missing an answer. You get your problem nailed down, so you don't try to keep up when you're only half-prepared.

I hate tests. If they didn't make such a big thing out of it I wouldn't mind the work, but I feel like I'm in a police court. There are so many rules about not cheating and doing things just so, that I get too bothered to think straight. What should I do about this?

Adam

Some schools have a way of policing tests which is so rigid that you forget that tests are supposed to be part of learning. Your teacher has to conform to the school policies, but she may be able to help you cope with it. You might also get extra help preparing for your exams. Go over the material with your parents, or get them to drill you if it is the kind of exam that asks for a lot of facts. Being sure of your preparation will make you more confident. When you sit down to take the exam, remind yourself that this isn't a trial; you are simply being asked to write down some of the stuff you have learned.

We get too much homework. It takes me hours and hours to do mine. Often I don't get to bed until eleven-thirty or twelve. Is this fair?

Susan

It sure isn't good for you to get so little sleep. The point of the homework is to get practice in what you learned during school. It should give you time for extra reading and the opportunity to do independent work, writing papers or doing projects. The only way to learn math, for instance, is to *do* math. Teachers have a good idea how much time you are expected to take to do homework. Check on this. If it takes you a lot longer, the trouble must be with the way you work. Do you have a good, quiet, private place to work at home? Do you really study all this time or do you daydream, make trips to the refrigerator, file your nails, and catch a bit of TV?

If you are sure you concentrate and don't get interrupted, and it still takes you longer than everyone else in your class, you need some fast help in work-study techniques. Ask at school for this.

My parents never will help me with my homework. If I ask a question, they say, "Go look it up." Or if I can't figure something out they say, "You ought to have learned that in school." Other kids' parents practically do their kids' homework for them. Shouldn't mine help me more?

Bud

Parents ought to be available, of course, but mostly to provide encouragement. Too much help is probably worse than too little. Instead of giving you answers, parents can show you where you can find them for yourselves — such as in the dictionary. Instead of working problems for you, they can help you try to remember how it was done in school. If this doesn't work, you are much better off taking the unfinished problem to your teacher and finding out again how to do it. The methods used in school today are different from those used in your parents' day. They may not be able to do things the same way. If you need a lot of help from your parents, something's wrong at the school end of things. You may not understand your assignments well.

I get along pretty well in most subjects, but I get failing marks in math. My father is quite upset; he says this will hurt my chances of getting into college. He tries to help me but it doesn't seem to help. My teacher tries, too, but I go sort of blank when he is explaining, and can't take it in and then he gets mad and says I'm not concentrating. Aren't there some people who just can't do math? Why do I have to take it when I'm not going to study science, anyway?

J.R.

Anyone of average intelligence is potentially able to "do" math, but it is a subject that many people get learning "blocks" about.

There are fewer colleges now that expect kids to be good at everything. No one is. Everyone should realize this. If your father is worrying that a failing grade will hurt college opportunity for you, he would do well to turn his energies toward getting you some extra help.

> *You're my last hope. I'm debating whether or not to run away. Last spring my report card wasn't so hot. I've just got another that is worse. My mother says, "Try harder next time," but my father has blown his top. I am being punished. I suppose I could do better in school, but he makes me so mad I just want to run away. I want to forget school and my parents, too. Should I?*
>
> *Miles*

It wouldn't decide anything. You have to fight the battle where the war is being waged — in school and at home.

When you get behind, your teachers get down on you, your parents get mad, and your own self-esteem takes a nose dive. Because you do badly, you hate school. Because you hate school, you do worse.

A three-way conference is in order, between you, your parents, and the school. It can help figure out how bad a slump you're in, how much of it is due to your age, whether you need extra help, what your parents' attitude toward marks is doing, and how much more effort you can reasonably be expected to make. This won't solve everything, but it could take a big load off your mind.

Teachers

It's pretty hard to be neutral about a person you spend so much time with and who has so much power over you. Most teachers take on the job because they want to work with kids, and most of you get along with them well — but not all.

When you are thinking about what kind of a person your teacher is and whether you like him or her, you need to watch out for something — projection. This is a way people have of transferring to the other fellow something that is really a problem of their own. Do you hate math? Then your math teacher seems like a lemon! Bored by French? Your French teacher's unfair! Dislike basketball? The coach is a bully!

We all do this. Even teachers. It is useful to recognize the projection trick and try to be honest about your real feelings.

Teachers come in all varieties like any other bunch of humans. What if you really do get a lemon? This is also part of education. You'll meet lemons in all kinds of situations, all your life. It helps to know how to get along with them without allowing their sourness to get under your skin and make you think less of yourself.

What if you have a crush on your teacher? This is okay, too, but again, it is useful to recognize it for what it is.

From your letters I gather that what you most want from teachers is understanding. What you like least is sarcasm. You'd rather have a teacher be fair than charming. Humor helps a lot, but unkind cuts do not. Control is desirable, but not by threats, temper, or screaming.

Most teachers would probably go along with this list, but now what about your behavior? Does it bring out humor and understanding in teachers? You are at an age where you tend to resist authority. Authority = teacher. Therefore you are capable of some first-class bitchiness yourselves. Don't expect that understanding to stretch too far.

I hate my science teacher! She's ugly and wears sloppy clothes and doesn't speak nicely to us at all. I have never liked science and this year we just aren't learning anything at all.

Alma

You have the cart before the horse. Your dislike of science is making you dislike your teacher. This is a good example of projection.

Being ugly and rumpled has nothing to do with being a bad or good teacher. Her manner of speaking probably is a result of your boredom and obvious dislike. Talk to her about your dissatisfaction and see if she'll find some project or reading that has special interest for you.

I'm in the seventh grade and I am sort of shy. Hardly anyone pays any attention to me, but that is not my problem. I don't get in too much trouble, but my teacher seems to dislike me. My girl friend isn't as smart as I am, so I tell her a lot of answers. In that class she usually gets B's or A's and I get D's or C's. I think this is unfair, don't you?

Thomas

Your teacher may have a pretty good idea of your girl friend's capabilities. When she surprises her with right answers, the teacher gives her credit for high achievement . . . for her. She knows she can expect more from you.

Teachers try hard not to play favorites, but all human beings are attracted more to some people than others. If you are shy, it must be hard for her to know you well.

And then there's another likely explanation: she knows darn well you're helping your girl cheat.

Myself and some other kids in my class are very bad. We have a softy teacher. She can't keep control of our class. There are four kids in the class who are very good. How come? Because they have self-control, but we don't.

The way we act would get us killed in other classes. We said at first, "Man, we're going to have a blast." Now we're getting sick of this. We never learn a thing. Help us know how to keep control of ourselves.

El 50

It is natural to see how much you can get away with. But this isn't the only desire you have to follow. You have a choice: Which gives you more satisfaction, getting a rise out of your teacher or conducting yourself in a way that lets you respect yourself?

Take another look at this teacher. Sure, she isn't strong. Not all adults are. It is important to learn that you can manipulate people on the basis of their weaknesses. At the same time, it is important to realize that people who are weak in one area usually have strengths in another. Perhaps this woman can be a kind and effective teacher — *if* you give her the chance.

You and your buddies may find out that it feels good to be acting mature enough to take advantage of a person's strengths, rather than their weaknesses.

There's this teacher here that none of us like. He's strict and he rules his class with an iron hand. Even the boys

are afraid of him. I will say that we are learning a lot of
geometry, but we wish he'd be nice and friendlier to us.

Concerned Student

A teacher doesn't have to be popular to do his job well. It is
nice to have a jolly teacher, but it is also satisfying to learn a
lot and have respect for the teacher who can teach well.

You don't seem to feel that your geometry teacher is unfair,
or unnecessarily rough, intimidating, shaming, or scornful. I
think you'd better just accept the situation.

One of my teachers picks on me. She calls on me twice
as often as anybody else. The other kids have noticed it.
What shall I do?

Marcia

Ask her. Maybe she doesn't realize she is doing it. Or maybe
she thinks you aren't well prepared and is trying to check up.
Then again, you may be one of those kids a class needs, whose
responses are listened to by other students. Kids like this are
great mood creators in a class and a teacher uses them to advantage. If that is the case, it should make you feel pretty good.

Help! Most of the boys in my class have no use for
teachers, but I seem to have this thing about one of them.
She is young and really pretty and I can't stop thinking
about her. She doesn't act differently toward me than
anyone else, but I keep thinking perhaps she likes me be-
cause she gives me extra stuff to do. I like this, but I'm so
afraid the guys will find out how I feel.

Eighth Grade Nut

Bet you a dollar a lot of your friends admire her, too. And like you, they keep it a secret.

Your teacher is handling this wisely, it seems. She is being impartial. She's giving you those extra tasks to burn up some of your excess energy, which will make it easier for you to handle this crush.

You are wise, too, to keep this under your hat. By next year you will be thinking more about girls your own age, most likely.

I have a very nice teacher whom I like a lot, and he seems to like me. I'm a junior. Other teachers object to our flip attitude toward each other, especially the older teachers. He does not favor me in class, but after school in the corridors, he helps me with problems I don't understand. I have tried avoiding him, but I am taking a tough course and need help, and he is the only teacher who can give it to me. The flip tone comes naturally when I am talking to him. What can I do?

Teacher's Pet

It is very nice to know a teacher well enough to get past the usual teacher-student formalities and be friendly and relaxed with him. It isn't so good, though, when things get too personal, and I think this is your problem. A "flip tone" is a way of flirting. It's normal for girls to have crushes on male teachers, but I think you're a little beyond that. This must be a young teacher who is not experienced in handling these situations.

Teachers naturally respond to some kids more than to others, but practiced teachers control this tendency. Everyone resents an obvious show of favoritism.

Your teacher would be wise not to be alone with you much.

Can't you do your extra work in the class instead of out in the corridors? And if this course is so hard, what happens to the rest of the kids who need help?

Speaking in class, cheating, and skipping

Many of you are bothered by having to stand up and answer questions in front of all the other kids. It's part of shyness. The more informal atmosphere many schools have now is helping, but there is still a lot of stammering and embarrassment.

Cheating is a common occurrence in school, more than many people realize. Kids who wouldn't cheat outside of school feel it is okay to do it in class because so many others do. Some junior high school teachers estimate that 33 per cent of their students cheat. Others go as high as 90 per cent. So it's a problem all right, and one teachers are more aware of than you think. It's pretty obvious from up front. But it isn't necessarily easy to know what to do about it from up there.

And then there is good old playing hooky. Who doesn't like to get away from trouble? As for outright running away, I get letters from many who have considered it, but none from kids who have done it. When someone runs away, it is no longer a school problem. It is a whole raft of other problems.

I'm calm enough with my friends, but when a teacher asks me a question I jump up, blurt it out, and slam back in my seat. I'd like to be more calm and confident. I try, but I'm always failing. All the socially confident kids say I'm a nut. Others say I'm a good kid. What am I going to do when I start to date boys?

Nervous Wreck

Most teen-agers go through a time of being very unconfident. Even those "socially mature" people must be shakier than they look or they wouldn't bother to cut you down as a "nut." They do this to build themselves up.

You may be more nervous than others your age because you are more critical of yourself. You feel you should be more poised, more mature, more perfect. Confidence will come as you get more maturity and take a kinder view of yourself.

Listen to those friends who say you are a good kid, and pat yourself on the back for getting up and answering the questions, even though you're scared. Your confidence is built a little bit each time you do it.

One other thing — dating boys isn't a bit like public speaking.

In school a friend of mine is always cheating on tests. We are supposed to correct our own with a red pen, and she has a pen that is red at the top and blue at the bottom. When we correct, she flips the pen to the blue side and puts all the correct answers in. I am mad because it isn't fair to everyone else. I really don't want to tell on her. What do you think?

Mad

You can't really tell on her. You'd hate being a tattletale and your friends would think you were a traitor to your kind.

It's infuriating to see someone getting away with murder. She isn't learning much, though, and will probably get caught. Her good scores probably don't raise the class point average enough to make much difference. I think this is her problem — not yours.

*We two are in the seventh grade and usually get A's.
Some other kids in the room are taking advantage of us.
They always cheat off our papers and we are afraid we
will get caught giving them the answers. If we don't give
them the answers, they get mad, and we don't want to lose
them as friends. We try to avoid them during tests, but
they keep pestering us and we think the teachers are
beginning to get suspicious. We don't know how to handle
this, and are afraid we are only hurting ourselves.*

I.L. & L.H.

No, they are hurting themselves, too. Cheating whittles away
a person's self-respect. But you'll lose their respect, too, if you
let them push you around.

If you stop and think about it, they need your friendship as
much as you need theirs, if not more. You have the right to
tell them you would like them better if they stopped copying
your work. Suggest that the axe is about to fall on all of you, so
why not quit now while everyone is in the clear.

Do you think it's so bad to cheat?

Vin

I don't think cheating is harmless. Once or twice doesn't
make you a criminal. You get a little less honest, however, each
time you do it. And honesty is a better way of life — at least I
think so. Do you like people you can't trust?

*I had a test I hadn't studied for, so I skipped school.
Like a dope, I went to a store to get a hot dog and someone saw me and turned me in.*

I was suspended for two days for "playing hooky." I stayed home and had a ball. What kind of a dopey punishment is that?

B.L.

It is a routine punishment. It doesn't seem logical, perhaps, but it goes on your record, where it doesn't look very good. Most kids mind this more than they are willing to admit.

A lot of kids skip school once, or maybe twice, and once or twice doesn't do irreparable damage. I think parents are wise to put a suspension to some use other than having a ball. Running away from your problem didn't solve anything, did it?

*

I have had arguments with a lot of you about which attitude is right: Is it worthwhile to work hard now for something that will reward you later on, or is it only worthwhile doing a thing if it gives you pleasure right now, while you're doing it?

You accuse me of being caught up in the old Puritan ethic of "work for work's sake." And I think you are caught up in a demand for "instant gratification." As with most arguments, the truth probably lies somewhere in the middle.

I agree with you that education doesn't have to be grim and rigid. You've come up with lots of refreshing new ideas, which many schools are now trying, to make education more interesting, imaginative, relevant, informal, spontaneous, and honest. I think you still have to expect to do hard work in school. There are dangers in seeing everything in terms of the pleasure principle.

5

Attracting the Opposite Sex

Dear Beth,
Help! I have developed a real liking for a girl in my
class, and suddenly I can't think of anything to say to her.
I feel like such a fool! What's the matter with me?

How *do* you get the person you like to like you back? That is
just about topic number one in early adolescence.

What makes it so hard? Boys and girls used to be able to
talk comfortably together. Now, suddenly, the girls have
begun to stick out in front and the boys have begun to notice
it and — *zap* — there you are in a bind, curious, fascinated,
but terribly self-conscious around each other. You used to kid
and wrestle and trip each other up. Now it's hard to know
if you should even say hi.

The great social game is about to begin, but you don't know
the rules. In our age sex and social life are being outlined and
dissected in book after book, but nobody is teaching the things
that young teen-agers need to know.

How do you tell when somebody likes you? If you're a girl
and a boy hits you, does that mean he does like you? Funnily

enough, it may. If you're a boy and a girl giggles every time you look at her, does that mean she thinks you're a boob? No. Probably she likes you but is excited and nervous.

You want to know how to ask for a date, and how to accept. You want to know if it's okay for a girl to call first. You'd like to be cool about it all, but it takes experience. You haven't had it yet. Perhaps you can get some tips reading about what these other kids bumped into when they first started on this special relationship with the opposite sex.

Making contact

How do you get to meet boys, anyway? Some of the girls in our school just seem to know all the boys, but I never get to meet any of them.

Eager

Some girls do just seem to know boys, but most of them have to work at it. Girls who are unusually relaxed socially have boys flocking around because they make everyone feel at ease. Other girls hang around in a group that knows a gang of boys. It's easier to approach boys in a group than all alone. You might look into this, and see if there is a congenial bunch of girls you can get to know.

For direct action, find out where the boys go, and follow. If you like the looks of a boy who plays football, you can't join the squad, but you can be an enthusiastic spectator, and get his attention that way. Investigate the co-ed sports at your school. Also other activities — chorus or drama, perhaps — which boys do. This is a good approach, because people meet easily when they are doing something together, not just formally trying to get acquainted.

Look for after-school action, too. If there is a popular hang-out, grab a couple of girl friends and hang out in it.

But the best meeting place of all is right under your feet every day — the school halls. A friendly hi in the corridor has started more good friendships than any other technique devised by man.

There are some girls in my class I think are really cute. I'd like to get to know them. What should I do first?

Bob

Smile. Grin. Wave. Say hi. They are probably dying to get to know you, too, and if you create the opening, will jump through it like seals at the circus.

I don't know how to start with a girl when I like her. I don't drive yet, so I can't ask anyone out and expect her to walk. I can think of a few girls I'd like to get past the "Hi" stage with, but they seem to think I'm just being friendly when I try to get someplace with them. Where do I start?

I don't want anyone to think I'm scared, but there is one girl I care a lot for.

T.D.C.

Then stick close to her, and do the things you *can* do to-gether. For after-school stuff, take a bus, or get a parent to drive you.

Girls understand about the license problem. They will settle for whatever transportation is possible, because they think it is fun to be with the boys who like them.

I go to an all-girls' school. I'm desperate for a little fun. It's girls, girls, girls, night and day, and I don't see how I'll ever get a date. They are good kids, but we are almost fifteen, and going crazy.

Abby

Doesn't your school have mixers? If not, form a student committee and try to organize some.

Investigate after-school opportunities. Does your community have a teen center? What about church clubs; YWCA (they have dances); 4-H (it's co-ed)? Perhaps you can find a volunteer job that gets you into contact with boys. Or a part-time job, especially one serving food, where you are apt to meet many people.

Take up a sport. Wangle invitations home from friends who have brothers.

Get together with some friends from school, and give a party, picnic, barbecue, or dance. What boys? All their brothers, each of whom will bring one or two friends.

Why don't the parents of boys respect a girl who calls their son? I call a lot of boys, and they don't mind. The other night after I called my boy friend my mother got mad and said girls don't do things like that. Why?

Caller

In the old days, girls didn't. It was considered "forward," and a girl who did it was "fresh" or even "brazen." Girls were supposed to be helpless and wait prettily for boys to take all the positive steps. Now girls are allowed to take steps of their own. Boys don't lose respect for them if they don't overdo it, so their parents shouldn't either.

During vacation my girl friend and I met two boys from a distant town. They seemed to like us, and we all had fun together.

We forgot to give them our phone numbers, and haven't heard from them. We have their addresses. Should we write, or leave things as they are?

D.V. and F.R.

Don't underestimate the ability of boys to use phone books or ask questions. However, if you think they are so shy they need prodding, drop them a line — once. If there's no reaction, drop the whole idea.

Why do people always say a girl shouldn't chase a boy? My girl chased me, and I'm really glad she did. If she hadn't, look what I'd be missing now!

Hooked and Happy

Girls have always chased boys. The successful ones just don't let it show.

How do you act with a person you really like?

I have a boy friend I like very much. His best friend told me he likes me too. But I'm not so sure anymore. Often he

*hits me and kicks and calls me names. But, say ten min-
utes later, when he wants something, he becomes so nice!
What do you think?*

Sal

Sometimes it is clear as a bell that the person you like likes you.
Often, though, it's clear as mud. When kids are shy or unsure,
they may show their affection in very peculiar ways.

Now I don't think Sal's boy friend really does like her. I
think he's using her, and he's a stinker. But stranger things
have happened.

You probably feel yourself that you don't know how to act
around someone you really like a lot. You don't want to make
a fool of yourself, and gush all over the place. But you want to
be sure they get the message that you think they are pretty nice.

*I like a new boy that moved into our neighborhood. I
play with his sister. Now the boy is teasing me and sometimes smiling at me. I don't know if he really likes me. We
are the same age. What should I do or say?*

Georgie

Whatever you are doing and saying now, keep doing and
saying. When a boy is teasing and smiling, he is liking.

*I like my girl friend's brother and he likes me. When I
visit her, he is usually there, which is good, only I don't
know how to act. A girl acts differently when she is with
her boy friend, but there I am with my girl friend and my
boy friend. I try to be myself, but I get giddy. How can I
get through to him that I like him without devoting my*

complete attention to him? I don't want to sit there with a gushy smile on my face all the time.

Cupid's Target

Of course you can't be as unself-conscious around your boy friend as you are with your girl friend, but you have the right idea in trying to be yourself as much as you can. If you really like the boy, it is going to show anyway, without the gushy smile. When you are very attracted to a person, you tend to point in that direction like a bird dog. You always know where that person is, hear what he says, and notice how he feels. There are subtle things your body does you aren't even aware of. He may not be conscious of them either, but he'll be reacting to them just the same.

Go on being pleasant and attractive to both. If the boy has a sneaker for you, he'll read your message, loud and clear.

I have a girl friend. When I ask her if she likes me, she never answers. What shall I do?

Miserable

Stop asking. Actions speak louder than words. If she acts as if she likes you, what difference does it make what she says?

Just recently a boy has called me up and asked me for a date. This is the first time a boy has ever shown even the least little bit of interest in me. As much as I hated to, I had to say no, because my parents say I'm too young. They say that before dating I must go out in groups. Is fourteen too young for single dating? Is it wrong for a boy to call on the same night he wishes to take you out?

Desperate

Many, many parents feel that fourteen is too young for single dating. You can be *asked* by one boy, but travel in a group, or at least on a double date. It is easier to learn how to be with a boy if you start off with other kids along.

I don't see why a boy can't call you up that same day, for some spontaneous fun. Naturally, for a dance or more formal party, he should ask you ahead of time.

First dates

It takes a lot of nerve to ask a girl out for the first time. It takes a lot of nerve to accept, even though you're dying to. This is just the beginning, however. Now you are starting on your first date, and all is unknown — what to wear, what to say, how to act.

You may be too shy to talk. Your excitement may make you a flood of words. Few can take such a big moment in stride, so remember, whatever your reaction, everyone else has gone through a similar flap. Forgive yourself if you make a few mistakes. It may be touch and go now, but you are all going to have a wonderful time when you've dated enough to know what you're about. The thing is — you have to start.

How old do you think a girl should be to be allowed to go out on a date in a car with a boy? I'm fifteen and my parents won't let my date pick me up. It is very unfair!
Footsore

There are two problems. One is the boy's ability to drive, the other his intentions toward you. Many teen-agers are excellent drivers. Others, more immature, try to show what big shots they are behind the wheel. Your date's personality is more important than his statistical age.

Then there are the boys who use their cars for mobile make-out parlors. Many parents believe that a girl can handle an incipient Romeo better by the time she is sixteen. Those who feel that their daughters can cope let them go earlier.

I just had my first real date. It should have been perfect. Jim's neat, the movie was excellent, and afterward he took me to get a hamburger. But halfway through the movie I began to need to go to the bathroom. I couldn't get up the nerve to mention it, and after a while I couldn't think of anything else. By the time Jim got me home, I was sure I would explode. I had the car door open already and jumped out yelling "Thanks" as I ran up the steps.

Of course, he hasn't called back. Why was I such a dope? How can I let him know I really like him?

B.J.

Everyone makes mistakes when they do something for the first time. When you're nervous, you always "have to go." Everyone does, and most people feel shy about it with others they don't know well. Your gang must have a stock phrase for this event; use that next time.

Tell your friends what happened so that word will filter back to Jim that your problem was high water pressure, not disappointment with him. You're still interested. You hope he'll give you another chance.

I took a girl out for the first time the other night. We went to a dance at school. She's very popular and while we were dancing she kept waving and talking to the other guys. I couldn't get her attention much. Even when my dad was taking us home, she talked more to him than me. I never could think of anything interesting to say.

I asked her to go to a game next week, but she said she couldn't. Shall I ask her again?

Dan

I wouldn't. I think she is more sophisticated than you. You'll develop more poise as you date more, but why not start out with girls more your speed socially rather than the school queen? They will be happier to be with you and not so busy getting attention from the masses all the time.

First date — DISASTER. I took a girl I really like to a picnic, and made such an ass of myself. I dropped her thermos and broke it before we even left her home. I burned myself cooking the hamburgers, and just missed slamming her hand in the car door.

Everyone laughed their heads off, but she was really cool about everything. I want to ask her out again, but don't know if I should. What do you think?

Bungler

Ask. She can always say no. But I bet she won't. She was cool because she is an understanding person who knows that boys, like girls, can be terribly ill at ease on their first date. This is what makes them awkward. She can take it in stride if you do. Give her the chance.

I have liked a boy for a long time, and now he has asked me out, but my mother feels she should know him. He objects to meeting her. How can I change his mind?

Troubles

Ask him for dinner and serve his favorite food. If he still won't come, drop him. A decent guy knows a girl's mother is entitled to look him over.

There is a girl I really like, but she isn't that good-looking. I took her to a square dance, and she got herself up in a kind of weird outfit and my friends made fun of her. After a while I was so ashamed I made a couple of bum remarks myself. Since I hurt her, she has stopped speaking to me. She really is a good person, and I'd like to get her back. What should I do?

Ashamed

Apologize. Whether you want her back or not, you still should let her know that you are sorry.

Before you try to win her over — and she may not be able to forgive such a devastating experience — visualize future dates with her, and ask yourself how you will behave. Will her good qualities be more important to you than the ribbings you will get from your friends? Be sure you can take this in stride so you won't subject her to another letdown.

What if you don't want dates right now?

Perhaps many of the kids in your class are going on dates but you don't really feel like it yet. You get a lot of pressure.

Others kid you. Maybe even your parents are asking why you don't go out with that cute kid next door. But you just don't want to. Are you okay?

Yes. You are. It doesn't help much for people to say, "Relax. This will all work out." But maybe these facts will bolster your confidence in yourself. You are perfectly normal. You just need a little more time for growing up. Being with the opposite sex will not be as strange as you fear. You'll find your opposite numbers are pretty much like you — human beings — in most respects. And they will be inexperienced too, and not expecting much sophistication from you.

I am thirteen years old. There's this boy who likes me very much. He's in the ninth grade and is fifteen. I like him too, but every time I'm alone with him, I get scared and try to run away.

The problem is he's a great kid and really cares a lot for me. There's nothing actually to be afraid of that I can think of. Please give me some advice.

Runaway

The idea of having a boy friend is exciting. To have a boy so much older like you is especially so. So you like the idea and you like the boy — but you're not ready for it yet. Don't rush yourself. You've got lots and lots of time.

I can't make up my mind about boys. I don't want to go steady, but I like to go to parties. I'm not even sure I want a date, yet there are times when I wish there was some boy who seemed to know that I exist.

Sometimes I go into a depression because boys don't

show any interest in me. Is there anything wrong with a fourteen-year-old girl who doesn't want boys to notice her and then turns around and wishes they would?

Switcher

No, there's nothing wrong. Most girls have this feeling at some time in early adolescence. You realize you are supposed to start having boys in your social life. You like the idea all right, but when you come close to the fact, you feel insecure. You're afraid you aren't grown-up enough yet to know how to act on an actual date. So you backtrack.

Boys can sense your reluctance just now. When you are willing to date, they'll sense that, too. Then they will discover your existence quite rapidly.

I don't go out with any special girl. We have a gang and I see lots of girls, and we have fun together, but people keep kidding me about not having a girl friend. I'm fifteen. Should I have one?

Allen

No need. You are having a good lesson in getting to know girls just the way you are. For now.

Puppy love

Okay. You have got yourself together. Your nervousness has vanished, you've had a lot of dates and had some wonderful times. You have found someone you really care about, and you think you may be in love. What happens next?

I'm fifteen and a half and in love with a boy for the first time. I have had boy friends before, but never felt this way about any of them. My parents think it is okay, but they keep calling it "puppy love." What is puppy love, and how is it different from real love?

Puppy

Puppy love implies a temporary infatuation, and this is often the case with love between young people who are still immature and inexperienced. It isn't a derogatory term, or shouldn't be, for puppy love is very important. If you never had it, how would you get the experience necessary for mature love? So don't feel insulted.

Love at fifteen seems very real, and it is. But you don't want to be surprised when it does turn out to be temporary. Ninety-nine times out of a hundred, the boy you love at fifteen won't be the one you settle on for the rest of your life. This is good. You need to know several different boys before you can make a good choice of a permanent partner.

The difference between puppy love and real love, besides permanence, is in the capacity of the lovers for mutual understanding and caring. Real love doesn't just happen — it grows after lots of time together, developing deep compassion, trust, and consideration. It is the greatest thing in life, and worth years of hard work.

Meantime, enjoy your puppy love. You are ready to go steady. Just try not to get so deeply involved, however, that you forget you are still rather young.

6

Sex and Love

Dear Beth,
    Lately I find myself thinking sexy thoughts all the time.
I read these magazines that I know are junk, but I can't
stop myself. I daydream about it, too. I've never been
this kind of girl before. Do you think I will turn into some
kind of sex fiend?

It is a temptation to call this chapter "The Sensuous Teen-Ager." Every other age seems to have its Sensuous book, but teen-agers deserve first claim to the subject. Adolescence is when sex strikes full blast; the sex urge is stronger then than at any other time.

Your glands now make you aware of sex. Your equipment for sex is coming of age and new drives *force* you to think about it.

Like the girl in the letter above, you may be bothered by your thoughts. This grown-up body is new to you. You have generalized feelings of excitement you don't understand. You have specific feelings that you understand all too well — they are frankly sexual. How do you handle all this?

There used to be strict moral codes that helped. They said, more or less, "You may learn a few facts, but you will wait until you are grown-up to use them." Now the codes are loosening. It is harder to know what is right.

What about love? When you first are aware of your own sex drive, the whole business can seem raw and crude and not related to love at all. Figuring out the part sex does play in mature love is one of a teen-ager's most important jobs.

This chapter is to help you sort out some of your thoughts and feelings about love and sex. It includes the change in attitudes toward sex in today's society, and also some common misconceptions and deviations from normal sexuality. It doesn't deal with physiology, as you most likely can learn that in school. It doesn't deal with lovemaking either, as that is such a big part of your life it needs a chapter of its own.

How to tell the difference

My parents keep telling me that a girl should wait for sex until she is old enough for love. What's the difference?
Young Girl

Take a bull in a pasture. He sees a cow. Charge! His feeling is all physical. It's pure sex.

Take a boy. He knows a girl he likes a lot. He likes to think about how beautiful she is. He idealizes her — tells others she is so bright, so clever, so kind. He feels tenderness toward her — likes to help her do her homework, or give her presents. He likes to hug and kiss her, too, but the term romantic love refers to his affection for her and not to his physical attraction.

Sex with people is more complicated than with animals. Reproduction is the furthest thing from your mind when you hold your boy friend's hand at the movies. Just the same, handholding is step A in a long chain of events that leads to step Z — reproduction.

Mature love between men and women isn't separate from sex, but it combines sex with other feelings. When you love someone, you admire and respect them. You want to care for them, sympathize with them, and make them feel good. You desire them sexually, but you also care for their welfare as much as you do your own.

Attitudes toward sex

There is a strong breeze of honesty sweeping through the country trying to blow away some of the Victorian unnaturalness about sex. The old idea that sex was necessary, but not something to be enjoyed, certainly didn't do much for human happiness.

However, along with a healthy frankness about sex has come a tidal wave of books and movies and ads and theories and manuals about sex that threatens to engulf us. The new free attitude is therefore a mixed blessing.

Morals are created by a society to set down rules of behavior that will make the most people the most comfortable, most of the time. As times change, parts of the moral code get out of date. Usually the basis of the code still makes sense, for people don't change fundamentally from century to century.

The basis of the sex code is to keep man monogamous. This is because a family makes the best place to raise children from infancy to adolescence. A lot of people are worried that the new sexual freedom is threatening family life.

This new freedom also threatens the rules that used to help protect teen-agers from their strong sexual urges. You have to develop your own rules, but you still need some guidelines. It is wise to look at both the old and the new ideas about sex to see which ones can help you decide the best way for you to behave.

The other day I asked my mother a simple question about sex, and she got all flustered and could hardly answer me. I knew she would, but I had no one else to ask. Why are some parents so uptight talking about sex?

Sandra

Your parents didn't invent this reaction. Sex is such a powerful urge that man has felt it necessary to control it with taboos, all through history.

In our country, the Puritan idea of purity was reinforced by Victorian prudishness, so it's no wonder many people felt squeamish about sex. Do you realize Victorian ladies couldn't even say "leg"? They had to say "limb" instead.

Many people grow up with the notion that there is something dirty about sex, because they got confused about sex and bathroom functions when they were very small. The organs for both are very close together, so when parents scold kids for lapses in toilet training, and say "dirty" and "nasty," the children often get the idea that sex is nasty too.

And parents rightly want to protect their kids from overstimulation about sex. They fear they might lose control. They remember when *they* were adolescents, and worried very much about this.

All these points show why hesitancy in talking about sex is very natural. You probably feel some reticence yourself when you try to talk about it with your mother. But at least you are both trying. Future generations may be able to drop all this shame and embarrassment to a much greater degree. And that will be a big help.

I have been arguing with my girl friend about sex. I say people have been hung up on the idea that sex is bad and dirty and dangerous for too long. They never practiced what they preached anyway. So it is high time the old moral junk was tossed out, and we thought of sex the way we do other natural things. Like food. You get hungry — you eat.

My girl friend doesn't agree. She was brought up very strictly and says the moral laws are good. Most of them anyway. Which of us do you think is right?

Bobby

Both. It's true that lots of people have been "hung up," and because they were afraid, they couldn't have the happy sex life a normal couple should enjoy. Frigidity and impotence will be greatly reduced when we all feel more comfortable and relaxed about sex.

It's true that there is a lot of hypocrisy, too, and that it's bad. The sex spree in our country is on, with movies and books and magazines all seeming to say, "Sex is great! Get with it!" This message is beamed at teen-agers as well as adults. But what does society say to kids? "Uh unh. You have to wait. Sex is not for you." This creates a dilemma. Returning sex to a natural place in the scheme of things will help a lot.

New birth control methods and ease of abortion have made sex much freer. But freedom can be carried too far. Sex that has no more significance than drinking a glass of water misses the boat. If you reduce sex to a mechanical process, you dehumanize it. People are capable of stronger bonds than animals. Sex between a man and woman who truly love each other in all the many meanings of the word can reach a level of tenderness and total communication and bliss that is one of mankind's greatest joys. Don't settle for less.

Your girl friend is right in thinking that many of the moral codes about sex make practical sense. It makes sense for kids to wait for sufficient maturity instead of rushing into sex. Each person has to develop the right code for himself. He must also respect another's "right" code. It may be different from his. So don't try to persuade your girl to act freer than she thinks she should.

How kids learn about sex

Children try to find out about sex the way they learn about everything else, by watching and asking, by touching and doing. But this runs them smack into a lot of trouble. We treat sex as a private affair, so they can't watch. It's a highly charged topic, too, so we don't answer their questions very well. They aren't supposed to experiment with sex — Mother takes a fit when they play doctor — so that road is blocked, too.

All this mystery and excitement is instantly felt by little

kids. They say to themselves, "Hmm. There must be something pretty special about this!" They are more curious than ever. So they turn to their brother or sister or friend to get some answers. Whispered conversations and peeks in the bathroom give some ideas about reproduction, but ideas that are often distorted, confusing, or downright frightening.

Well, how can you learn? From your parents, because they are the first models you have of people loving each other and their children. In most cases they can also answer your questions more frankly as you get older. If not — and many parents feel very uncomfortable about this — you may have to turn to books. There are excellent books on sex written just for teen-agers on most public library shelves.

And then there is sex education in school. This has caused a big commotion in many places. Some people felt it was a bad idea; others felt that it didn't work well. But so long as so many kids have bum information or are really upset about sex, it seems to me most important that someone be setting them straight. At the moment, school programs seem to be the best way we have found.

I don't have a question exactly, but I wish you'd print something about the way parents teach kids about sex. The old story about the birds and the bees just doesn't work! My parents are very embarrassed talking about sex, and they told me the stuff about the pollen. They told me other things, too, but I was sort of confused. Now I have talked to friends, and we have a sex course in school, so I know what's what, but don't you think it is dumb to tell kids about animals when they want to know about people?

Hates Pollen

You are absolutely right. It makes me wonder why some boys don't think they have to fly over their wives in some mysterious way, or girls worry that their husband is going to ram pollen up their nose. Wild!

Parents should tell children what the facts are simply and honestly, and using the correct terms. Fortunately, embarrassment about sex is easing, and parents of the future will be able to talk much more comfortably with their kids. Then the bees and flowers will be left to do their own thing with all that pollen.

We have some sex education in school, but I'm always too scared to ask questions. I'd like to ask my mother, but she never talks about such things. I think she's more scared than me. There are a couple of things I want to know. What can I do?

'Fraid to Ask

If it is too painful for you and your mother to talk, get a good book about sex written for teen-agers, like Dr. Spock's *A Teenager's Guide to Life and Love.*

If you don't find your answer, you can use the book as a tool for getting your mother to talk. Ask her opinion of the part in the book that comes closest to the subject you need to find out about.

My parents don't like it that we are getting sex education in school. My mother says parents have the right to teach their own kids the facts of life, and the stuff we get is just teaching us "to be bad." Do you think so? What can I do?

Worried

Parents certainly have the right to teach their children and they can continue to do so, even if the school does have a sex education program. If your mother is worried about what is being taught, I hope she will visit your school and discuss the program with the teachers.

Learning about sex does not make kids promiscuous. Some kids don't even know how babies are made. They can get in trouble through sheer ignorance. The school programs are designed to make sure they have the facts straight, and to tell them what problems are likely to arise and how to deal with them.

How do you feel about your own sexuality?

No matter how "natural" it seemed before to be a girl or a boy, thoughts and emotions that come flooding over you now are very different from anything you have ever experienced. You can be curious, but ashamed at the same time; you can be excited, but scared; eager for new experiences, but timid about trying. One thing you can't be is oblivious. The opposite sex is on your mind, and that's that.

All this doesn't happen exactly the same way to everyone. Some kids start sooner, some later. Boys feel differently from girls. Some teen-agers get crushes and others never even daydream. Everyone goes through some forceful changes during puberty; that's what it's all about. And everyone has private fears, and wonders if he is the same as others, or is having unique, unusual reactions.

The following letters are about different feelings some kids have had in wrestling with their own sexuality for the first time.

I have been having some dreams about sex that are just horrible. I couldn't begin to tell anyone. They are so disgusting I hate myself. Is this natural for a teen-age boy, or am I sick, do you think?

W.P.

It's natural. You are now mature enough to have strong sex urges for the first time. With these come thoughts about sex. How do you know what to do about them, when you have never had such thoughts before?

When you were little, it was considered inappropriate for you to think about sex. Now it is actually necessary for you to think about it, for you have to learn how to deal with your sexuality.

Dreams happen because you believe some of the thoughts you have are "bad." You don't dare let yourself think them, so they pop up in your dreams. Don't be scared by this. The nicest, most normal teens have these dreams, sometimes about members of their own family, even their mothers. It shocks them, too.

These dreams have nothing to do with being a sex maniac. Often they bring up childhood ideas or misconceptions about sex which can then be discarded. As you get used to being more adult, your thoughts and feelings about sex will become sorted out. Your dreams will have done their work, and they will occur less frequently.

I just adore my cousin. He's seven years older than I am, and I know he has a girl friend, but whenever he comes to our house he gives me a special big hug and kiss,

*and says I'm his favorite. I really love him. I dream
about him every night.*

Thirteen and Foolish

You've got a crush. This is one of the steps in learning how
to love. You don't really expect your cousin to love you back
in a romantic way — you just enjoy dreaming about it.

Many girls have crushes on popular singers and actors. They
are testing out love affairs in their imagination before getting
involved with real boys.

It's useful to have crushes. But it's good to recognize them
for what they are. I wouldn't tell your cousin how much you
adore him; it might embarrass you both.

*I am fourteen and met a boy at a dance who I loved
from the very first minute. I think about him night and
day. I'd do anything for him. Mother says this is just an
infatuation, and I have to be grown-up to know what real
love is. Is this true?*

In Love

Teen-agers are capable of very compelling feelings of love.
When you feel you would "do anything" for another, this is
the caring and sharing aspect of mature love that takes it beyond a purely physical relationship.

Infatuation implies a temporary relationship. When you fall
in love suddenly, you think you have found your ideal. Everyone carries around an ideal in his or her imagination and is
ready to fall in love with anyone who seems to match it. But
you don't know this boy very well yet. Perhaps he will turn

out to live up to your image of the perfect boy. Then your infatuation may develop into real love. If he doesn't match up, though, you will turn to someone else.

Teen-agers change boy and girl friends a lot. Your taste changes. Your ideals may change too. You will be better equipped emotionally when you're more mature and have had more experience to develop a love that is constant and enduring.

Is there a basic difference between men and women so far as sex is concerned?

M.N.

Popular opinion is changing very rapidly on this point. It used to be thought that maleness and femaleness were built into people because of their anatomies. Now we believe a lot of behavior patterns are fixed onto them by social attitudes about male and female roles. We don't have the whole answer yet.

Certainly there are misconceptions. Do you have to be six foot two and built like a fullback to be virile? No. You can be five-four and scrawny and still be virile in every way.

Men do have bigger bodies than women, usually, and are stronger physically. They were traditionally the fighters, hunters, providers, and protectors. Women traditionally stayed home, bore and raised children, and followed orders. In many cultures, men were considered sexually aggressive and women submissive. In some, women were not even supposed to be interested in sex. Therefore people came to believe that men had more "sex drive."

Now there is medical and physiological evidence to show that a woman's sexual drive and sexual pleasure are just as strong as a man's. But there are some differences. Male and female hormones are different. Since a man's equipment for sex is on the outside, he is more quickly aroused than a woman. His sex impulse is more urgent, and more focused in his genitals.

A woman's primary sex organs are internal. Her sexual pleasure is spread more over her whole body, and is slower to be aroused in her genitals. Also, a woman's sexual desire is more wrapped up in the necessity of being loved in the more general sense of that word. She can mechanically be a sex part-ner without ever being aroused at all. Not so a man.

It is probably a biological fact that the male of the species is the initiator. What difference does it make who starts the process, so long as both sexes are able to enjoy it equally? The old Victorian idea that a nice woman "never feels a thing" is, of course, bunk.

My mother hates me to date. She always warns me, "Boys are only after one thing!" She's divorced, and I think she hates men. The boys I know don't act like sex fiends. She says, "Just wait!" Are boys more out for sex than girls?

K.G.

In some ways they are. A boy's sexual feelings are closer to the surface, and so he thinks about sex sooner and more frankly than most girls. Many teen-age boys feel they have to prove their manhood by being very aggressive. And it is even true that a boy is more likely than a girl to have a strictly sexual affair.

But boys certainly aren't after "only one thing." They can be fully as tender and romantic as you. What it boils down to is that boys are most likely to make the first pass. This does NOT mean they are going to become passionate and uncontrollable menaces. Most boys won't run roughshod over you. You can stop them any time you want to by saying no. If necessary, scorn them.

Your mother has had an unfortunate experience, and you must realize how this colors her opinion of men. Don't let it affect yours.

I want boys to kiss me, but when they do, I don't like it at all. I feel as if I'm going to explode. I get shaky and can hardly breathe. I push them away, and this makes them mad. I think I'm afraid of sex, but I don't want to be unpopular. What am I so scared of?

Kay

Several things, and all perfectly understandable in a young teen.

When you were little you probably got the idea that sex wasn't "nice." Good little girls don't think about it. Now that you are big, and find that nice girls *do* think about sex, you still feel a little guilty about it.

Girls are taught to be leery of sex because girls are the ones who can be most hurt; they can get pregnant. Even though a kiss is a far cry from this possibility, sex seems so dangerous to you that even the kiss is threatening.

You may be afraid the kiss will get your boy friend so excited you won't be able to stop him from going too far.

Finally, kisses arouse sexual feelings in you, and you are scared by the power of these emotions. They may not be felt in a way you expect, either, but as "exploding" or "shaking."

All your fears are due to the newness of this experience in your life. When you get used to dating, you'll feel fine about it. Instead of shakiness, you'll feel great pleasure. But don't feel you have to kiss boys until you're good and ready.

Homosexuality

What most people mean by "normal sex" is sex that has as its ultimate aim intercourse with a person of the opposite sex. Sometimes techniques of lovemaking may be unusual, but so long as the two people involved are happy with them, their sex life is normal.

Homosexuality is sexual love for a person of the same sex. Therefore it doesn't meet most people's definition of normal. We all know it exists. It is much in the news at the moment, because many people want to change the current view of homosexuality as something vile, shameful, and illegal.

In trying to win acceptance, some homosexuals, both male and female, have been crying out that their kind of sex life is not abnormal. "Look at the Greeks!" they say, and some even suggest that people who haven't loved a member of the same sex are missing something.

However, most people do not regard homosexuality as desirable. The very idea terrifies them. I get scores and scores of letters from boys and girls who are afraid they have an unnatural affection for someone of their own sex. I think parents would be astounded if they knew how often their children worry about this.

You may feel better when you realize that everyone has the

potential for both homosexual and heterosexual feelings. In adolescence, all kinds of feelings come to the surface temporarily, and when you can understand this, you will see that most of your fears are groundless.

I'm a junior in high school and have a problem about another boy who plays in the band with me. He has been after me to come home with him and rehearse. I'd like to do this, except a lot of the guys say this boy is a homosexual. His voice hasn't changed and he hasn't much fuzz on his face. I sure don't want to get the reputation of running around with a fairy. What do you think?

Ken

I think your friends are jumping to conclusions. Some boys develop much more slowly than the average in the beard and voice-changing departments. It's a dirty trick to brand someone as a "fairy" when he is just a late bloomer. What a terrible blow to his ego!

Tell your friends that looks don't tell much about homosexuality. A bearded, muscular, masculine-looking fellow can be a homosexual, and a slender man with a weak physique and hairless chin be a regular tiger with the ladies. Give the boy a chance.

I'm a girl going on fourteen, and there is this girl in school I have a crush on. What gets me is when I am with my friends I act all right, but when I see her I go crazy. Why do I go through torture when I am in the same room as she is?

I dress, look like, talk, act, and even think like a boy.

My friends even call me Tarzan. Convince me I'm a girl
— not a boy!

Tarzan

You don't need to worry about being a tomboy. That's a
fine thing to be when you're young. It teaches you to be a good
sport and will help you understand the male point of view when
you start going out with boys.

And you will. Don't worry about that either. One thing
that happens in adolescence is that you look back to see what
things from the past you are going to keep, and what should be
discarded as childish. You even revive old feelings, like the way
you used to love your mother — but you have this affection for
some other female, in your case a girl in school. You feel so
strongly that you "go through torture." But it's temporary.
Soon you will feel excitement about a boy instead.

It's not unusual, when you have such a strong crush, to worry
that you are a lesbian. You want me to convince you that you're
normal, and you are. Crushes just mean you aren't quite ready
to be the feminine half of a boy-girl romance yet — that's all.

*I'm not a particularly masculine type. I know this, and
I don't like it, but up to now I've had a normal enough
life. I mean, I have a girl friend and everything. The
other night when I was coming home on the bus this man
kept staring at me. He got off when I did and grabbed my
arm and wanted me to go someplace with him. I finally
ran home, but God, was I scared! If a guy like that likes
me, does it mean I'm a latent homosexual?*

Unnerved

Absolutely not. This was *his* problem, not yours.

A man who tries to pick up boys or adolescents is very unfortunate, but he is a man to steer clear of, as you did. Actually, you don't even need to run away, as these homosexuals are usually very anxious and timid, and a resounding "No" on the boy's part will discourage them fast.

Why are some people homosexuals? Are they born that way? How can you tell if you are?

C.C.

Everyone has a degree of homosexuality in his make-up, and some may be born with more than others. Most psychologists feel that the way you are brought up rather than your physiology determines your sexuality.

Most boys love and admire their fathers. By imitating them, they learn how to be men. If a boy's father was *extremely* harsh or cold, or if his mother was *extremely* overprotective and spoiled him, this might keep him from wanting to be a man. He might decide it is safer or nicer to be a woman. Therefore he acts like one when he is grown, even preferring to be loved by another man, as women are.

In the same way, a girl whose father is *unusually* close to her and/or whose relationship with her mother is *very* unsatisfactory may identify with her father instead of her mother and try to imitate him. She will walk and talk like a man, and may even wear men's clothes (though today it is hard to tell the difference). Sexually, she feels like a man and wants to love a woman.

Those *extremelys* and *verys* are set in italic type because teen-agers are often very uncomfortable and even angry with their parents and vice versa. This is temporary and part of normal growing up. No matter how furious you get at your mother or father, it is not affecting your sex growth. This was set much earlier in childhood.

Confirmed homosexuals recognize their feelings quite early in adolescence. They know they are different. Sooner or later they will engage in homosexual behavior.

A person who has a lot of doubts about his sexual identity, however, will struggle. Many teen-agers who are preoccupied with homosexuality actually are anxious about sexuality in general. If you ever have acute anxiety, it is an excellent idea to get professional help in sorting out your thinking.

Is homosexuality all bad? Some of my friends say it is only bad because it is illegal. They even seem to be interested in it.

L.T.

The shame that society heaps on people who are homosexual through no fault of their own is bad and harmful. Present laws that support this attitude should be altered. Nevertheless, the laws aren't the only drawback to homosexuality. I doubt that many people would deliberately opt for this kind of sexuality if they had free choice.

As for your friends' being "interested in it," some young people feel they have to experiment with all kinds of love. The fact that homosexuality should not be derided doesn't mean it is an experience we all need to try.

Other deviations

When people say "sexual deviance," they usually mean homo-sexuality, but there are other ways in which sexuality can be different from normal. A "Peeping Tom," for instance, is a guy who never got past the childhood phase of getting sexual excitement from watching other people get undressed. Perhaps he was overstimulated by such sights when he was little (score one point for the old moral code, which would try to prevent this). Anyhow, he is hung up right there, and hasn't progressed to adult sex.

Some people can fall in love only with a person they feel is inferior. You may have read about an heiress who marries the family chauffeur. A Ph.D. may be capable of feeling sexual love only for a prostitute. Usually these people are convinced that sex is unworthy, so they can't bring themselves to associate it with anyone they admire or feel is their equal.

This is the age of armchair psychologists. We all like to ana-lyze each other, and put people in categories. We fling labels around such as "queer," "nympho," and "masochist" much too freely. Often when you are a teen-ager, one aspect of sexu-ality may be temporarily exaggerated. In sex, as in every other road to adulthood, there is no one, straight, inflexible path to perfection. We learn by trial and error. So you need to be tolerant of a certain amount of trial and error.

You certainly want to be aware that sexual behavior can get out of line, and to avoid this strenuously when you meet it. But you need to be realistic about what is abnormal. This is a darn good argument for knowing and respecting people before you get intimate. Kids whom you find to be wholesome and kind and understanding in every other way are not likely to be "perverts." They may surprise you with sudden or inept advances, but you can chalk this up to experience if you know them well enough as friends. If you don't, you haven't got anything to base your judgment on.

My violin teacher is an old man. I used to like my lessons, but lately he has been getting very affectionate with me. It's so embarrassing! If I make a mistake, he pats my fanny. Sometimes he says I'm holding the fiddle wrong, and he'll put his arms around me to show me how. He's completely bald and has bad teeth and bad breath and I think he's going to kiss me. He's pathetic, and I don't want to hurt him, but I just hate this! What shall I do?

Frieda

You could stop him in his tracks by saying, "Please don't be fresh." But this may be too difficult. You are probably too polite, and were taught that older people know how to behave themselves.

You are right that his advances are pathetic. Probably he has trouble finding reciprocal love with someone his age. He is frustrated, so he loses his inhibitions when he's close to an attractive young girl. It is kind of you to feel sorry for him, but you shouldn't put up with the harassment. It's not dangerous, but thoroughly uncomfortable.

Tell your mother. After all, you can't learn much when your teacher fiddles around this way.

I can hardly bear to write this, but I just have to tell somebody. Two days ago my girl friend and I were walking home when this grungy-looking man stepped up and said he had to show us something. Like dopes, we followed him around the corner, and he went into an empty lot and unzipped his pants. We were so shocked we stood there like dummies. Then we ran and ran all the way home. My girl friend said she was sick all night. I'm afraid to go out. What makes a man do that? Do you think he wanted to hurt us? He never tried to touch us.

Kip

A man like this sure is frightening, but he isn't likely to harm you. He's frightened of sex himself and doesn't dare try it with a real girl, so he gets his kicks from exposing himself.

The best way to cope with someone like this is not to show you are afraid, but to tell him firmly to stop. You could even say, "I'm going to find a policeman." Keep your dignity. Walk away.

The thing is, he was bluffing. If he weren't scared himself, he wouldn't resort to such behavior. He wanted you to be frightened and run away. If you hadn't, it would have called his bluff.

There's a girl I'd like to date but my older brother says to stay away from her, she's a nymphomaniac. She's been out with a lot of guys, but I thought it was because she's such a dish. What makes a girl a nympho? Would she be bad for me?

Herb

A real nymphomaniac is a woman who keeps looking for new partners in sex because she can't seem to establish a satisfying relationship with any of them. She is always searching for her ideal, but always failing, because the trouble is inside herself. (A man who has this problem is called a Don Juan.)

I doubt that this "dish" is a nymphomaniac. She's more likely just a flirt who likes to play the field. Or she may be trying to prove she is lovable by making lots of conquests.

How could you be hurt by a girl like this? Even if she is a nympho, you can always say no. The only hurt you're likely to get is hurt feelings if you expect a very loyal friendship from her.

Obscenity and pornography

It's impossible not to run into some book or story or movie that is designed to shock you with lurid details of sexual excesses. Will obscene pictures hurt you? What should you do if you run across a bit of pornography? It would be stupid for me to tell you to turn your back on every racy magazine, or a deaf ear to every dirty joke. You couldn't avoid it all if you tried, and anyway, you probably don't want to. We all have curiosity about sex.

The thing to do is to use some discretion. You need to realize what a shallow picture of sex this stuff is really giving out. The human aspect of the sexual relationship is disregarded in pornography. It brutalizes something that ought to be tender and sensitive as well as exciting. So if you get all wrapped up in it you are getting a very one-sided view of sex.

The value of mechanical explanations about positions and sensuality training and all this contortionist jazz is exaggerated. People to whom sex comes naturally don't need this artificial hoopla. As a matter of fact, pornography is boring and empty compared to the richness of a relationship that unites tenderness and care and the fullness of human imagination with sex.

My mother caught me reading a "sexy" novel, and got very angry. When I asked her why, she said it would give me "bum ideas" about sex. I told her I wasn't taking it seriously and that I was reading it for amusement. She replied, "Sex isn't a laughing matter." I said she didn't seem to realize that there is much more freedom about sex than in her time. She said, "It's trash, and get it out of the house." Isn't she overreacting?

Harry

It depends a little on the book, but if it was real pornography, I think her statements are basically sound.

Victorian literature was throttled by prudishness and priggery, it's true, but pornography isn't the answer either.

Most pornography is sex that is peddled not to educate, but to make money. An adult can read about cruelty and violence and unusual practices if he wants to without much harm, but as young people haven't had experience in what normal and desirable sex is like, they can indeed get "bum ideas."

Furthermore, the authors of some of this stuff are mixed-up people who present distorted views of sex to satisfy some twisted ideas of their own.

I agree with your mother's point that making sex a laughing matter can be carried too far. It is natural to snicker about things that are private and exciting. Dirty jokes were told in ancient Rome, and didn't hurt the Roman kids. But to make a practice of treating lovemaking with low humor degrades it.

You want sex to be a valuable part of your life. It's your loss if you devalue it.

*

Sex is a complicated business. Often other emotions get tangled up in it — rivalry, fear, aggression, guilt, even hate, and how you feel about your mother and father. This brings many problems to adults as well as to teen-agers. These problems are being studied in depth nowadays, and reported on in books like the Kinsey Report and Masters and Johnson's study of sexual behavior. I see no point in going into such aspects of mature sexuality as frigidity and impotence. When you need this type of information you will do better to read it in these books for adults.

One point I do want to emphasize. All this talk about sensuality and prowess in lovemaking has made many kids rather scared. Boys are afraid they won't prove to be virile enough. Girls worry that their mates won't find them adequate or lovable. I want to reassure you. If you and your partner have such love that you really care about each other, and if you can communicate your real feelings and concerns to each other, you will surmount, almost surely, any difficulties that sex might present. And then you will have reached the ultimate in human commitment to another.

7

Going Steady

Dear Beth,
   I have been going steady with Greg for over a year.
We're both sixteen. My parents wish I'd go out with some
other boys, and sometimes I do too, 'cause I think we've be-
come sort of a habit with each other. But then I know that
none of the boys are half as nice as he is, so I don't want to
split up. Lately we've been fighting quite a lot. What
should I do about Greg?

Lots of parents do not think going steady is a good idea for
young teen-agers. Is it? It all depends on how mature you are,
and how seriously you take it.

If you are still pretty young, it isn't good to be out of cir-
culation too long. Kids who get too close and too involved
usually wind up in each other's arms. If you are fourteen or
fifteen, you aren't prepared emotionally to handle a lot of sex.
And this complication makes it pure hell when you break up.

Pressure to go steady these days is mighty heavy. In some
schools you are a real creep if you don't. This forces many kids
to grab at anyone who asks them, which is often a mistake. But

who can resist under the circumstances? So let's look at the good side of going steady.

There is the secure knowledge that you always have a date. And when things work out, it's just plain wonderful to know that you like someone and they like you back. Nothing does more for the ego. Realizing that you are a lovable person makes you feel that "all's right with the world." This can have surprising results. You may do better in school. You may even smile at your parents.

Everyone needs to be close to somebody. Learning to relate and developing mutual respect and confidence is a giant step in your growth. Having a steady gets you into more complicated social situations. Sex is part of it — a big part, but only part. Or should be, anyway. Companionship, having someone you can share your intimate thoughts and feelings with, is equally important.

Kids used to have to be pretty stiff and formal with each other at dances and parties. Now everything is informal, and you can be together as naturally as colts in a pasture. It helps you get to know each other better.

But one thing hasn't changed. All's still fair in love and war. Or is it? How fair do you have to be? You may be very surprised by how ruthless you feel when you are attracted to somebody and want their affection too. Getting that certain person, hanging on, and then perhaps letting go is what going steady is. It's topic number one in my mail and what these letters are all about.

I met a boy at a dance, and he bought me a Coke and danced almost every dance with me. At the end he asked me to go steady. I was afraid to say yes, because he was awkward and clumsy, and acted like an ape. When I didn't answer, he told me to think about it. I don't like him too much. What should I say and do?

Afraid

If you don't like him, say no. The point of going steady is to be with a person you *do* like. You haven't known this boy long enough to tell. If you want to find out, see him again. Maybe he is only awkward and clumsy because he's ill at ease at dances.

My boy friend is sixteen and I am fifteen and we respect each other and have lots of fun together. But a few weeks ago I began to feel that it was all one big dream. I seem to be in a fog. It isn't that he has suddenly forgotten me, because he is as nice as ever. I almost wish he weren't! What is making me feel this way?

Peculiar

You may feel, subconsciously, that you don't want to relate to one boy so exclusively. He is nice, so there is no rational reason to break up with him, but something is warning you against getting too serious just yet. This is perfectly normal. Girls your age ought to date different boys. You don't get so intense, and you can expand your knowledge of boys rather than just concentrate on one specimen.

I'm not the smartest student in the world. I have to hold down a part-time job, and to keep my marks up at the same time, I have to study a lot. The result is that I never have any free time. I figured I could get my social life later on, but my relatives feel I should start dating now. Since I

*don't have very much money, and don't know any girls very
well, I don't see how I can.*

Maury

You have to work hard *not* to meet girls in school, and there
are ways you can date that don't cost very much.

Listen to your relatives. They speak the truth. You need to
know the opposite sex in a variety of situations. Having a girl
friend is a great ego booster. Everyone needs this.

Stop hiding behind your books and your job. Get into cir-
culation. Make eyes at some of the cute girls out there in the
halls and see what develops.

*I am a college student and I don't date very much, but
there is one girl I have gone with off and on for five years.
I don't stay awake nights thinking about her, but then I
never seem to find another girl I like as well. Last spring
I didn't really think I loved her, but I'm sure we'll drift
back together when school starts. Do you think it's true
love after all?*

Don

Sounds to me more like true lethargy. Get off your duff and
find a girl who *does* keep you awake nights. You owe it to yourself.

How do you choose a "steady"?

A lot of factors contribute to your choice of friends. A boy
may like a girl because she talks a good game of ball, or has
freckles on her nose, or reminds him of his favorite movie ac-

tress, or just because he feels relaxed when he's around her. What other people think of your choice may make a lot of difference to you, especially in the early teen-age years. No one wants to be caught going steady with the class creep.

But what about the poor creep? How does he or she find a steady? Happily, fads change. And happily, too, kids get surer of their own tastes as they get older. You gain the courage to stand up for your own opinions. So almost every high school student is dating someone by the end of senior year.

Whom do you pick? If the girl you like is another boy's steady — possibly even your best friend's — is it okay to try to lure her away? Suppose two boys like you. How do you decide which to pick?

What if your boy friend is two years older? Four years older? Younger? Funny-looking? A different race or religion?

Learning to choose someone who will be compatible is a vital job for you. Mistakes teach you too, so don't feel you have failed if the person who at first excited you so much turns out, on closer acquaintance, to be a bore. You won't be excited by the same type another time. Finding out what you don't like is just as important as finding out what you do.

My best friend Anita has been dating Mike for months. Now Mike has started fooling with me. He calls up just to tell me what a good kid I am. I didn't start this on purpose, but I do like him.

He and Anita have now broken up, and everyone blames me. They say I stole Mike away from her, but is it my fault if he doesn't want to go with her anymore?

Accused

You must have been acting pretty receptive to Mike's attention, or he wouldn't have called you in the first place. These things happen. You can't agonize over it. But you also can't rationalize your behavior to make it look as if you were innocent.

Here's your choice. Go on seeing Mike, and put up with Anita's wrath, which is justified. Or give up Mike and hope he will go back to Anita . . . which is unlikely.

There is a girl in my class in school that I really dig, and I know for sure she likes me. I want to ask her out, but she is going with another boy already. From what I hear, she isn't that crazy about him. Should I ask her, or forget about it?

Other Admirer

Tell her that you want to ask her and you wonder whether she would be mad if you did. This leaves the decision up to her — where it has to be.

I like two boys a whole lot. Peter has been my boy friend for ages, but Hal has been liking me for about a month. I've asked many friends what I should do. One says stick with Peter. Others say switch to Hal. Now I'm asking you. What should I do?

Becky

Ask Becky. She is the only one who can tell whom she really likes.

I go steady with a boy I like very much, but when I am invited to a boy-girl party I start worrying. He has a great personality but is fat and awkward. I'm afraid the kids will make fun of us. I am not worried for myself, but he is sensitive and shy and is in bad need of confidence in himself. He even refers to himself as a "big oaf." If they kid him, he may walk out on me. Should I take my chances, or stay home?

Help

Take your chances. Staying at home will kill the affair after a while anyway. Start at very small gatherings, where you know the kids well and can ask your friends not to make remarks. If that goes well, go on to bigger parties. Your confidence in this boy's likableness is the best help he can possibly get.

I am fourteen but I like a boy who is sixteen, almost seventeen. My family and friends say I am mature and able to keep things under control. Do you think I'm too young for him?

Mlle

Many seventeen-year-old boys don't need so much controlling, because they have got beyond the stage where they have to make passes at every girl to prove what big men they are. An older boy is more interested in a relationship that shares many activities — dancing, games, movies, socializing, and just talking. He can understand that a younger girl needs to go very slowly in the making-out department. On the other hand, there are some sixteen- or seventeen-year-old boys who would want to go further than you are ready for.

It boils down to the boy's character. If this boy seems mature and understanding, you should get along fine.

I am sixteen and my boy friend is twenty-six. He's in the service, and when he came home on leave at Christmas, he was very affectionate with me. My mother says he is too old. I don't agree. There are eight years between her and my father, and I don't see why two more years than that could make so much difference.

Judy

At your age, ten years is a huge difference. A man of twenty-six is getting ready to settle down and raise a family. A girl of sixteen ought to be meeting all kinds of boys and learning how to pick her mate. She should also be having lots of teen-age fun. Girls who marry too early often feel gypped out of their childhood. Teen-age divorce rates are high. If you were twenty-six and he thirty-six, ten years wouldn't make so much difference. You'd both be pretty mature. But you're not. Find a boy closer to your age.

I'm fourteen and my steady is sixteen and a half. I like her a lot, but my parents say she's too old for me. I myself think age doesn't matter. She's a better athlete than most boys my age.

Don

It depends what you mean by steady. There's no reason why you can't be friends with a girl, and fish and play ball, but if you're talking of social dating, then age can matter.

Your parents are afraid this girl will push you into a more intimate relationship than you're ready for. At sixteen and a half, most girls are ready for that. At fourteen, most boys aren't. But rates of maturity can vary widely, and you may be a very exceptional case. Just make sure you aren't trying to look big by going with an "older woman."

Dating kids of other faiths or races

I get lots of mail from kids who want to go steady with someone of a different race or religion. Interestingly, not one letter writer has ever asked if he or she *should* do this; they always say their parents forbid it, and what should they do about that?

I have found no answer to the bind this gets us into. Should I ever advise a person to disobey his or her parents? A full and frank discussion by parents and their teen-agers would be much better. The only way they could reach any agreement would be to air their motives and their fears and try to understand each other's point of view.

One trouble is that when a teen-age girl dates a boy who isn't the same race or doesn't go to the same church, parental reaction is immediate. They review, usually with a lot of steam, all the reasons why a marriage between the two wouldn't work. They forbid or put great restrictions on the relationship. But the kids are talking about dating, not a wedding. Is this teen-age relationship more likely to end in marriage than the last one? Or the next one? For ninety-nine times out of a hundred there *will* be a next one.

Teen-agers shift steadies quite a lot. The more violent the parents' opposition, the more likely they are to turn up the volume on what was originally just another of their teen-ager's many dating experiences.

There are issues in so-called "mixed" dating that you kids must face up to, also. If you know your parents will hit the ceiling when you're a Catholic and pick a steady who is a Baptist, how do you feel about that? Do you by any chance rather like the idea that this will shock your parents? That's not unusual for a teen-ager.

Or do you want to strike a blow against prejudice? It is great to fight bigotry, but this isn't necessarily a good basis for love.

Some people may feel that these arguments are in favor of prejudice and against change. Not so. People of all different faiths and races can get along perfectly well. The problems that intolerance creates will not part them if they really respect each other. But they need to admit the existence of these problems *before* they can build a solid relationship. Then they will have something going for them that can truly endure.

I know a very nice boy but my parents won't let me go steady with him because our religions are different. Don't you think this is wrong? Won't they make matters worse by not letting us see each other?

T.B.T.

I believe that strong faith is not destroyed by contact with other beliefs. Many people feel otherwise, however. Your parents think it is necessary to isolate their family within the confines of their own religion. You need to understand how they feel, just as they need to recognize your feelings that strict confinement can make teen-agers rebellious. When so many young people are concerned about increasing tolerance and understanding, I think this is one of the times when a parent is more likely to keep his child by letting him go.

It might help all of you to get together if you had a good frank talk with your clergyman.

I'm eighteen and Jewish. My family is very liberal, so I was terribly surprised at their objection to my going steady with a Catholic boy. I brought him home to meet them, and they were coldly polite. After he left they really lit into me about him, and we had a bitter fight. I am so hurt by their prejudice that I am seriously considering running off with this boy.

Judy

Hold on here! Your parents may be opposed to your boy friend's religion, but then again they may just not have liked him or may feel that your own motives are cloudy. Get to the bottom of their objections calmly, and not just on the basis of one big fight.

If they are opposed on straight religious grounds, you need to understand their beliefs, for much of this has been inculcated into you. Whether you accept it now or not, it will always be one factor in your make-up. Orthodox Jews, and people of other religions, too, oppose intermarriage as a threat to the preservation of their traditions. This is not a fact you can lightly brush aside.

Interfaith steadies break up sooner than those where the kids have the same religion. So do interfaith engagements. The divorce rate of these marriages is higher, too.

Interfaith marriages *can* work, yes, but it takes hard work, and you'd better believe it. The kinds of problems that you would face must be worked out before marriage, not after.

When you talk about eloping, you are talking rebellion. Even if you have good grounds to rebel, these are not good grounds for a successful marriage.

Black and white dating

Our country has shown lots of prejudice against other races and religions, but black people in America have been put apart and put down with more vehemence than any other minority group. Feelings still run high, to understate the case.

Prejudice is now really ebbing among young black and white kids. On many college campuses today, the sight of a black boy holding a white girl's hand draws no special attention. But when this couple strolls off campus and down Main Street, some heads will invariably turn.

Life magazine asked the Harris Poll to conduct a national survey on this situation in the spring of 1971. The results showed that three quarters of the people in this country feel that "no matter what older people and parents say, young people of different races are going to see each other socially and we'd better get used to it."

But are we used to it? Many young people are; older people still get upset. More than half of the people interviewed think parents should place restrictions on interracial dating. Only 11 per cent would allow kids under sixteen to have such a date. About 50 per cent would let older kids date interracially in groups, but not singly. They think kids should talk to their guidance counselor or clergyman first.

So there are still plenty of problems. The very zeal with which kids fight for racial equality can confuse the issue when it comes to dating. Both the black and the white kids may want so desperately to prove color doesn't matter that they have trouble knowing their true feelings about each other.

Status can be another roadblock. If you have the courage to date kids of a different race because you *really* like them, that's fine. But if you date them because it is the "cool" thing to do, that's just as biased as refusing to date them because of their race.

Then there are those God-awful myths about race. Black men are superstuds. White people have better brains. Black girls are more passionate. Miscegenation is a biological disaster. They are fables, unproved by any reliable tests, but they still hang on to affect some people's thinking.

Mixed dating is fraught with troubles. There is great reluctance on the part of parents, both black and white. But more and more black and white kids are going steady just the same.

I'm sixteen years old, white, and have an eighteen-year-old boy friend who is black. I've known him since I was twelve. His family is very nice, and I baby-sit for the younger kids. My parents finally realized this boy and I are getting serious about each other, and have forbidden me to date him anymore. I tried to get through to my mother, but she won't listen to me. I can't support their theory of separation.

I talked to my boy friend about it, and we just don't know what to do. I have had plenty of other dates, but I like this boy better than any of them. He feels the same. Please don't write that I should just meet him at occasional little parties, or have fleeting conversations about the weather as we pass on the street. What should we do?

Renee

You can't deny that there is a lot of bigotry in this country. The way your parents feel may be wrong, but it is the way most parents feel about mixed dating now. You have to look at this squarely and see what the significance is to you.

A large part of parents' reaction is fear for their children's happiness. The boy's parents quite likely feel much the same way, though parents don't usually try to protect a son so much as a daughter. What parents fear is that mixed dating will lead to mixed marriage, and they know that mixed marriages in this country today are difficult.

See if you can't get your parents to go with you to talk this out with your clergyman, or some other person skilled in human relations. This could help you all get your real feelings out in the open where you can deal with them constructively.

I'm a junior, black, and I want to date a white girl in my school. My parents don't want this. They say it's wrong to date anyone you can't marry; it could just be leading her on; and they certainly hope I don't plan to marry a white girl.

I'm not thinking of marrying anyone. I just want to take this girl out a few times. Do you see anything wrong with that?

Henry

I see that your parents want very much to save you from getting hurt. Mixed couples are still subjected to quite a lot of harassment. One can't blame them for wanting to spare you this. However, I believe you are old enough to know what you're doing and how your friends feel, and that you wouldn't want to date this girl if it were going to be unacceptable to your classmates. I think your parents should trust your judgment.

I have a black boy friend and my mother and father are always talking to me about how I must be very careful because it would be so difficult if we should ever decide to marry. We are just going steady now, but I feel as if my parents were pushing me into something much more serious. I need some informed advice about what happens to a black-white marriage, and what the chances are that it can work out.

Muriel

One important thing that happens to such a marriage is that other people react to it — the parents-in-law, and friends and neighbors, and even total strangers. If you live in a place that disapproves of interracial marriages, you may be subjected to a lot of abuse. This can get you into the miserable situation of blaming each other for the unpleasantness.

The attitudes of husband and wife are crucial, of course. What are your deep-down convictions about racial differences? It would be almost impossible for some of the mud being slung around not to wash off on both of you. If you have doubts about whiteness or blackness, these feelings may rise to become a wedge between you in times of strain.

Sometimes blacks and whites marry each other for social or even neurotic reasons. People who have emotional hang-ups and can't get close to others sometimes marry someone of another race so they can say to themselves, "I don't need to get close to them anyway. After all, they're *different* from me."

Some people marry to shock society, to rebel against parental pressure, to rise up the social ladder, to dominate or be dominated by the other person. Many couples marry because they love each other deeply, but you have to be dead sure this *is* the reason. The other motives are not healthy ones for marriage.

Difference in background makes any marriage hard. The greater the difference, the narrower the fields you have to move in in terms of friends, places to live, jobs, and especially in terms of child raising. This last is uppermost in everyone's mind.

By current definition, the children of black and white parents are black. But they will have white grandparents as well as black ones, and possibly white cousins, too. So these children can be terribly confused about who they are.

A man and wife go into marriage willingly. They volunteer to take on the added burdens of race problems. If they have great love and resilience, they make it work. But their children have not volunteered. As a prospective parent, you would have to think realistically about what it is going to be like for them.

To say this is "racist propaganda" and "things will all work out" is shortsighted. Nothing is gained by putting off facing the real issues until after marriage.

If you and your boy friend reach a point of seriously planning marriage, I think you would benefit from talking to other mixed couples who have married, and especially those who have children. This is where you would get really "informed advice."

Breaking up

A high percentage of teen-age relationships break up. So who makes the break? If it's mutual there's usually no problem.

But if only one of you is disillusioned or feeling tied down, or has found a more exciting prospect, then there is a crisis.

If you were tough and heartless, you could break the news easily. "Beat it!" you would say, and let the hurt feelings fall where they may. But few people are that self-centered. You worry a lot about each other. In fact, sometimes it is just because you *are* concerned about damaging your ex's ego that you act much tougher than you are. To screw up enough nerve to deliver the bad news that you know is going to hurt, you try to convince yourself the other person is a jerk; then you can let them have it, but good.

This is common, but not admirable. There is no painless way to break up. Swallow the fact that you are going to inflict heartache. Be willing to suffer yourself as a consequence. Then you can manage it honestly.

Present the news gently, on neutral ground. Be sorry, and admit your part of the fault freely, but don't grovel. If you have found a new romance, it means the old one had some flaws. It's mainly a question of incompatibility.

Say you have given the matter a lot of thought (you'd better) and you know this is best for both of you. Then break clean. If your ex tries to win you back, don't equivocate. It is easier to make this break once than several times.

If you are the one who is being jilted, this is one of the toughest experiences you'll ever have. It hurts your heart, and it hurts your ego, too. A large part of the pain you feel is wounded pride. But don't overdramatize your situation. You need to learn how to cope with setbacks. Plenty of emotional hurts will come your way in life.

Make a quick recovery. Get the word out that you are soon going to be available, and not gloomily nursing a broken heart for months. Use the good part of the experience you had to build something even better with the next attractive person who swings into your orbit.

I've gone with a boy for five months, and up until a few days ago, I thought he really loved me. Now I have found out that he went with four other girls during this time. He hasn't called all weekend. I know it sounds dumb to say this at fifteen, but I love him. I think he wants to stop going with me. What should I do?

Hopeless

Sometimes a boy can get caught up in a date with another girl, even though he is going steady with someone else. So can a girl. It might be doing a favor for a friend, or a kind of a tentative experiment, but it isn't really two-timing. A boy who dates four other girls, however, is simply announcing, loud and clear, that he isn't in love with you.

All you can do is acknowledge it. It isn't a bit easy, but you have no choice. The sooner you face it, the sooner you will be free to make new arrangements.

I have been going with a girl with no problems for quite a while. Now she has me confused. Whenever I ask her to do anything, she always has to go home, or baby-sit. I don't know if it is coincidence or if she is trying to give me a hint.

Rejectee

The latter, I'm afraid. If it were just coincidence, she'd follow the turn-down with a suggestion for some other time you could get together.

*I went with the same girl all last year. Suddenly, I have
flipped over someone else. She likes me too. Now how am
I going to explain this to my old girl friend?*

Sid

You are going to explain it in person. It takes guts to face
the anger and hurt you are bound to cause, but it is a whole
lot kinder than writing or phoning.

You are going to explain it immediately. She deserves the
chance to look for somebody new herself.

And you are going to be tactful. You don't have to rub it in
that you have found a new girl friend. Tell her you really
enjoyed the times you had, but it is time for you both to branch
out. She may not believe this, but it lets her save face.

And don't go around telling your friends she's a loser. Be
man enough to leave her with her rating intact.

*How do you get over thinking about the boy you lost? I
cry myself to sleep every night. I think I shall always love
him!*

Lost

Of course you do! If it was a good thing you had going, it
deserves to be regretted. But you will be able to forget this boy
just as soon as you get interested in another one. It is hard to
believe that you'll ever feel like looking at another boy when
you keep saying to yourself, "It isn't true! He'll change his
mind and come back to me." Your ego is right in there pitch-
ing, too: "How could he *do* this to me?"

He did, though. You may have done it yourself to other guys.
If you haven't, you probably will. Precious few girls go straight

through adolescence to marriage with the same boy. Even now, .09 per cent of you is on the lookout for a likely prospect.

Don't be ashamed of feeling bad. But keep tuned in to that .09 per cent at the same time.

8

Lovemaking

Dear Beth,

I like this boy very much and I'm pretty sure he likes me. We've gone to parties together and we make out. At every party he goes a little further. I can feel his hands inching up. And when he does, half of me says yes, and half of me says no. When I don't let him, I wish I had. Even though we have gone out quite a bit, nothing serious has happened. Please tell me what to do.

The desire to get close to someone gets stronger and stronger now that you are an adolescent. If nature endowed you with all this drive, why shouldn't you exercise it all you want? Why wait?

This is assumed to be the Big Issue about lovemaking. It *is* imperative to understand why a mature love includes devotion and sympathy as well as passion. This is what lifts lovemaking above animal sexuality and makes it a rich human experience.

Parents worry about you going too far too soon. You worry about it too. But this isn't the only issue in lovemaking. With lots of you the problem isn't how to stop but how to get started in the first place.

Everyone knows how to kiss, more or less. You've been kissed by your mothers and fathers since you were born. But this kind of kissing is different from erotic kissing. It doesn't help you know how to kiss your girl good-night for the first time.

When you are a teen-ager you are supposed to be learning about love. To do this, you will be finding out what sexual feeling is like, and how to relate it to the other aspects of love, tenderness, and understanding. This doesn't mean to hurl yourself at every boy who comes your way to "test love." Far from it. But it is important not to be ashamed of thinking about sex, and the part it will play in your future as a wife and mother.

You need to learn how powerful the sex drive is and how to control it. Kissing is part of this learning. When you stop fearing that a single step like a kiss may lead to total loss of control, your reluctance will vanish like a Popsicle on a June day.

Everyone knows what petting is, too, more or less. But when should you start? And with whom? And how far should you go?

To hear some people talk you would think that all teen-agers are ready to make love at the drop of an Indian headband. The letters you write show, on the contrary, much hesitancy and uncertainty about this new stage in your life.

Kissing

I am thirteen and would like to know how old a girl should be to be kissed by a boy.

Wondering

Plenty of boys and girls try an experimental kiss at nine or ten, to see what all the fuss is about. It seems like blah, because they are too young. A quick kiss at thirteen doesn't do you any harm. But it is better to wait a few years for serious kissing, because that means a more serious kind of loving than you are prepared for. An exact age is impossible to give, because kids don't grow up at the same rate of speed.

I have been going with a boy for over two months. We are both sophomores in high school. Last night when he brought me home from the movies, he asked me if he could kiss me. I said no, but I was hoping he'd go ahead anyway. He didn't. If he asks me again, what shall I say?
                                                    Sweet Sixteen, Etc.

Say nothing. Smile. That should give him the encouragement to go ahead.

Lately I have been going to quite a few parties. We play the games that kids our age play. My mother told me to be careful, that you can catch a disease if you kiss too many girls. Can you? It is making me nervous.

                                                    Jack

Kissing isn't usually considered a medical problem. I suppose you could catch a cold, but do you think that's really what's making you nervous, or are you worried about the moral issues? Adolescence is the time when kids learn how to cope with things like whom to kiss and when. It's fun starting to get close to girls, but kind of scary, too. I think this is your real fear. Take heart! Thousands of boys kiss thousands of girls, every day, without any effect but pure pleasure.

Why is it that after you've kissed a boy, he just forgets about you? I should think a kiss would mean something to boys, but I guess it doesn't. What's your opinion?

Ipswich

My opinion is that a kiss means a lot to most boys. However, some kids of both sexes collect kisses the way desperadoes used to collect notches on their guns — to prove how sophisticated they are. I suspect you were kissed by one of these. Don't let it turn you off all boys. Wait to kiss a boy who really has a special feeling for you and he won't just forget you.

I am a nineteen-year-old girl, and have been going with a boy of twenty for close to five months. He means the world to me and we can talk about anything. But we've got a problem; he won't even kiss me. When I get close to him, he seems to shrink away from me. It upsets me that he can only show his affection for me in words.

Anxious

If your boy friend were fourteen or fifteen, his nervousness about getting close to a girl would be normal and natural; but at twenty, he should be beyond feeling so insecure about sex. See if you can persuade him to talk to a professional counselor about his fear of intimacy. He will be missing a lot if he goes through life just talking about love.

The guy I like very much, and who likes me, slips me his tongue. This has never happened with other boys I have dated, so what does it mean? It must have some meaning.

Surprised

Your guy is giving you a so-called French kiss. Frenchmen were supposed to be terrific lovemakers, and that's the reason for the name.

It means your boy friend finds you pretty nice and is getting more intimate with you. The next step will be petting. Your next step is to do some thinking about what limits you want to set for yourself.

Making out

Parents called it necking. Some call it petting. Your ancestors called it bundling. But whatever name you use, making out refers to those activities that come after a simple kiss and before the full and final act of sex.

It is extremely enjoyable. Nature made it fun with good reason, but this produces a quandary. The purpose of the whole exercise is, of course, reproduction, but this isn't suitable at all for teen-age kids — not, at any rate, in our society. The way making out works, though, is that the more you get, the more you want. And the further you go, the stronger is your desire to go further. Because "going all the way" presents a lot of problems, you have to find out when and how you can "halt."

Most people believe it isn't sensible to carry sex too far when you are a young teen-ager. On the other hand, most people expect that by mid or late adolescence you will be doing some petting. How do you decide what is the right amount for you?

Parents often say: "We didn't do all this necking when we were your age." Well, some of them didn't, but a lot of them did. The big difference is that in their day there was one very effective deterrent to help girls stop boys — fear of pregnancy. The Pill has changed the situation drastically. So kids are having to make the decision on their own, and "how far to go" is a burning question in my mailbox.

> *I'm fourteen and have been on many dates. My question is, at what age should two people start petting, either light or heavy? I say around sixteen, but the girl I am going with says now and is waiting to get started. I said I would light pet, and that's all. We finally agreed to ask you.*
>
> *Caught in the Middle*

You can't put a statistical age on the time to start. It depends on how old you are emotionally and physically plus how much experience you have had. There are big differences between individuals, and girls usually grow up in these ways faster than boys do. That's why your girl is saying "now" and you are saying "wait." I think more boys of fourteen would agree with you — that they are unprepared. If your girl really likes you, she won't push but will be willing to wait, at least for the heavy stuff, until you feel geared for it.

> *My father died when I was in the third grade and I can't talk to my mother about certain things. I have no one else*

to go to. I am at the age when you are expected to make out with kids if you like them. I don't think I would know how to do this if my life depended on it. Can you please tell me, or send me some information?

Scared

Making out starts with a kiss, and then a hug, and you will find you do know how to do that. It is as far as you need to go for quite a while, but you will find that the kisses get longer and the hugs get tighter as you date more often.

Somewhere in your midteens, depending on how fast you grow up and whether you meet someone you fall for really hard, you will probably want to go further. This isn't a thing most people learn out of books; it's built right into us. It will be hard not to, which is why it's not a good idea to make out too much with someone unless you love and respect them a lot. What you feel is your sexual urge, and it can be very strong. You have to learn to control it.

The more intense your making out becomes, the more you and your date will want to touch and fondle each other and in more intimate ways. This is "heavy petting." It is the preliminary lovemaking to serious sex. At this point, it really is extremely hard to stop yourself, especially (perhaps) for a boy.

Read some of the good books written for teen-agers about sex. You can find them at your public or school library. You need to know a lot about sex so you can make up your mind about the right way to behave, and not just drift into something you didn't intend.

How do you stop a boy from going too far without discouraging him completely? I'm very fond of the boy I go

*with and like him to kiss me, but lately he has begun, well,
you know, feeling me, and I think that's enough for now.*

Kitty

You can say no, but gently and with a smile that shows you
like him, even though you want him to stop. There are a lot
of ways to show a boy you like him besides making out.

He may not mind too much. Boys sort of feel they have to
keep trying to go a little further with a girl to prove they are
real men. When you say, "That's far enough," it shows him
he has proved his point, and can level off at that stage, confident
he has done his masculine thing for the time being.

If you stay friendly about your refusal, he shouldn't get mad.
If he does, he has got a childish notion about sex.

*I sure wish I knew how far a girl is supposed to let a guy
go. I have a boy friend I like a lot, and we kiss and make
out, but when he tries to go further, I always make him
stop. But then I have two girl friends who have gone all
the way. One is running around bragging about it. The
other feels terrible and says she only did it because she was
afraid she'd lose her boy friend if she didn't.*

*I don't want to lose my boy friend, but when he tries to
do certain things, I don't feel right about it. What do you
think is okay for a sixteen-year-old girl to do?*

Bette

I could give you a list like this:

At fourteen, hold hands.
At fifteen, a quick good-night kiss.

At sixteen, hugs and squeezes.

At seventeen, handle (with care) and kiss 'em on the tonsils.

But it would be ridiculous! All kids are different, and you have to develop your own rules to tell how far is far enough for you.

Part of being an adolescent is learning to accept intimacy. This sounds funny. You'd assume people would know how to make out instinctively, but having been told since they were tiny that they should do no such thing, kids really have to learn how to get close to the opposite sex.

The way you tell what is right is by how you feel. If you say to yourself, "I don't feel right about it," when your boy friend does certain things, then say no to him. This is your inner warning signal, and you are smart to listen to it. It is the conscience you have been developing all your life, with all the knowledge and morals about sex people have given you all these years. Unfortunately, it isn't always easy to hear this inner voice. There are lots of pressures on girls today to go further than they want to. Taboos used to protect girls from "getting into trouble." Now the restrictions are down and the opportunities are up. You have to make your own rules.

There is a natural urgency in the teen-age years to grow up as fast as possible. You want to try new things to act grown-up. If one partner has had more experience with sex, he or she will always try to urge the other to catch up. Don't be hurried. There is plenty of time for you ahead. Wait until you feel totally ready for each new step.

Your girl friend who brags about her exploits has fallen into the trap of thinking sex is some kind of status thing. Anyone who has to brag is a person who lacks confidence. She is making a big noise to hide the fact that she is unsure of herself. You don't have to delve into sex to be sophisticated. That's not what sex is for.

The other girl has let herself be blackmailed. This is too bad. She didn't listen to her own anxiety signals, and now she feels guilt and remorse.

As for you, I think you are doing just about right in holding the line.

The sex relationship

When you have a steady boy friend or girl friend, the attraction that pulls you together is enormous. Once you start getting intimate, the urgency of your sexual desire may overwhelm you. It is very, very hard to keep yourselves in check.

This is a new feeling for you, and you don't know how to control it. Though the taboos about sex are relaxing a great deal, there is still an illicit aspect to it that makes lovemaking all the more exciting.

If you give in to your urgent desires, and let out all the stops, you'll find it difficult to know how you really feel about each other. The sensations of lovemaking are so overpowering you will be hard put to know if you share mutual respect or just mutual desire for sexual gratification.

This matters because a pure sex relationship almost always results in progressive intimacy, and you wind up in bed. Perhaps you tell yourself this is all right because going too far is happening more often among teen-agers. It may be more common, but this does not make it any more sensible for you than it was for your grandmother.

I use the quaint expression "going too far" deliberately. Sexual intercourse *is* going too far for teen-agers in almost all cases. You are not mature enough to put the sexual part of love in its proper combination with other parts of love. If you hop into bed, on a wave of sexual urge, with a person you don't even respect very much, your own self-respect suffers. Most of you were raised to think that intercourse between teen-agers is wrong. So you will feel guilt, too, no matter how often you claim that it is right to fly in the face of convention.

A prolonged, serious sexual affair is all-engulfing. It ties you up when you ought to be free to explore many other facets of your teen-age world — and the other teen-agers in it.

I go steady with a boy without my parents' knowledge. Every time I am with him alone, all we do is make out. I don't think this is really wrong, but natural for two normal thirteen-year-olds. I've really fallen for this boy, and he tells me he loves me very much. I think we are both lonely kids who need someone to love. I know it is only a crush, but it is doing a lot of harm to my attitude toward things. Do you think what we are doing is wrong?

Flustered

I think you have a good head on your shoulders and have answered most of your own questions. It is natural for two lonely kids to seek solace in each other. You are alone together too much, and getting too intimate. Most kids of thirteen are trying an experimental kiss or two, and giggling a lot, but not much more. You don't really believe your behavior is normal. You are worried and feeling guilty, and your feelings are spoiling your attitude.

It is very hard to stop sex play when you have made it a habit, but if you two can branch out, make other friends, and stop seeing each other alone, I think you'll both be happier. See if you can help each other.

I am fourteen and my boy friend is fifteen. I don't know what he and I should do. A couple of weeks ago at his house we went up to his bedroom and we were making out. Then I got scared and made him stop. He said he was sorry and would never do it again. But next time we were at his house and got on his bed, he wanted to do even more. He didn't keep his promise.

The trouble is, I like him a lot. Should we just go on the way we have been, or should I stop seeing him, or what?

Nanine

He probably meant to keep his promise, but couldn't do it when you got on his bed and allowed him to start making out again. It probably didn't look to him as if you were sincere about not wanting to make out when you went to his bedroom.

Don't go on the way you have been or you will just drift into more and more serious sex, and you are both too young for this. I don't think it is wise to be in his house when there is nobody else there. Do your dating with other kids, or in public places where the opportunity to get so intimate can't come up.

A lot of girls feel that they have to put out a lot of sex in order to be popular. Well, let me say right now that when you give in to guys too much, your popularity takes a turn for the worse. You gain a reputation for being an "easy chick" and any guy you go out with will try to see how far he can get. Once word gets out (and believe me it travels fast) you'll never get a date with a "decent boy" because no matter how good the guy is basically, he is only human and susceptible to temptation. If you try to change, you will have to prove to each new date that you aren't "easy" anymore.

So don't give your date an opportunity to try anything in the first place. Don't say there's nothing you can do to stop him — a firm "no" usually does the job. A slap across the face will work as a last resort.

A boy will respect you only as much as you command his respect.

Teen-age Guy

I want to answer Teen-age Guy, who wrote you that putting out sex is all a girl's fault. I think it's as much the boy's fault. It seems to be always the girl who ends up with the bad reputation or sometimes even with a baby, while the boy gets off scot-free. I think sex before marriage is wrong, but it's wrong for both sexes, not just girls.

Girls say, "When you find a boy you want to get serious with, he won't like it if you've been handed around." What about a guy who has slept with every girl in town, or even just a few? Why should a "decent girl" date him? Why is it up to the girl not to give her date the opportunity?

Both the boy and girl have an equal part in the sex act. One doesn't play a greater part than the other.

I guess what I'm trying to say is that a boy has no right to expect a girl to be a virgin unless he can make the same claim. Which of us is right?

Eighteen-Year-Old Girl

You both are. The responsibility for a mutual act should be mutually shared. The double standard came into being because of women's vulnerability to becoming pregnant. The Pill has practically eliminated this. But the old standard dies hard.

Teen-age Guy has a point, too. Tradition has it that the boy tries to urge the girl to go ahead, and the girl is the one with more ability to "say when." He urges girls to use this ability.

You say both should use it. That's even better. Don't just inch along into the position where something serious does happen, and you heartily wish it hadn't.

9

Suppose You Get Pregnant?

Dear Beth,

I am fifteen and a half years old and going steady. I've been seeing this boy for three months and I like him very much.

One night (a month ago) he took me to a show and then home to meet his folks. Only they weren't there. I think he planned it that way. That did it! He took me up to his room, locked the doors, shut the lights, and put me on the bed. I wanted so much to stop him but I couldn't. He told me I'd like him a whole lot more. He's not an evil boy. He just wanted to prove his feelings.

Ever since that time I keep thinking I'm pregnant. I'm afraid to see a doctor, and twice as scared to tell my parents. I still have two years of school to finish, and a reputation to consider. Please tell me who I can tell. Please help.

Each year my mail contains more cries for help like this one. Why? How come so many girls get pregnant in spite of the Pill?

More and more young people feel that there is nothing morally wrong with sleeping together before marriage so long as they love each other. There is bound to be more pregnancy when there is more sex, because many teen-agers don't know how to get contraceptive devices, or don't dare.

There is still an incredible amount of ignorance, too. Some girls arrive at maternity homes, quite pregnant, but they don't even know how babies are made. There are still some mothers who let their daughters reach maturity without once mentioning sex to them. Sex education in school is only moderately successful.

Most kids do know something about it all, but they may drift into sex unintentionally, or just assume, "*That* won't happen to *me*." Often they are embarrassed to say no.

A few young people deliberately shun contraceptives as unnatural. They say they want to experience the "real thing," regardless of whether or not this produces a baby.

And then there are girls who actually want to get pregnant, consciously or unconsciously. They may be deeply angry at their parents, and getting pregnant is a foolproof way to get revenge. Or they may feel alienated from family and society, and so lonely that they look for sex to provide the love they are missing. They may even want a baby to have something of their own to love.

By far the majority of girls, however, hope and pray that they are *not* pregnant. They write to ask whether what they and their boy friend did was safe — and if not, how they can find out whether she is pregnant without anyone else knowing about it.

The purpose of this chapter is not to discuss the morality of the question. If a girl is pregnant, it is too late to say she shouldn't be. What she needs are facts, names, choices, and where to get help.

Here are several agencies that have branches in most cities. If one of them doesn't have the specific kind of help you need, they will gladly refer you to the place that does. They are listed here all together to avoid repetition of their names each time advice is wanted in the letters that follow.

Planned Parenthood League (especially for contraception)
Pregnancy Counseling Service (especially for testing and abortion)
Clergy Counseling (sometimes called Consultation) Service
Women's liberation organizations
Local hotlines and youth centers
Underground or student newspapers
U.S. or state public health clinics. Listed last because, though they wish to be helpful, the burden of bureaucracy tends to make them slower and more complicated.

If you can't find any of these, call your United Community Service or Red Feather headquarters to recommend an agency.

How to find out whether you are pregnant

I have a friend who wants to know if you can get pregnant without going all the way with a boy. She has done some pretty heavy petting, and she's worried. If the boy gets really excited, can something happen? Please tell it to me straight.

W.W.

Most heavy petting does not result in pregnancy, but there is always a chance that it might.

I assume that by heavy petting you mean stopping just short of intercourse, with emphasis on "just short." The boy would then have an ejaculation, probably in the vicinity of the vagina, not within it, so it is technically not intercourse. However, sperm are active, so there is always the chance that one will travel far enough to effect fertilization. And one is all it takes.

Seminal fluid is tremendously potent — 50,000 sperm per drop. Though the sperm die quickly if they aren't in a warm damp place, accidental impregnation has happened this way. The risk is too great to give sperm any kind of sporting chance to succeed.

I've been going steady with one boy for three years. It started with a good-night kiss, but then we got into some pretty heavy petting and finally we went all the way. If you have intercourse while in a period can you get pregnant? If so, can you have your period while pregnant? Please tell me. I love him and can't stop making love with him.

Frantic

Women don't usually get pregnant while they are menstruating, but it has happened.

A few women have regular monthly bleeding during pregnancy, though it is not usual. It is most common in the first couple of months.

I think you are probably not pregnant this time, but you'd better find out for sure. If you keep on making love, you will hit the jackpot soon, most likely. If you aren't going to stop, you need some kind of contraception.

I am fourteen and just had intercourse with a boy three days before my period. My friends tell me that I have a good chance of getting pregnant. Is that true?

Also, what are the symptoms of pregnancy? I wouldn't dare ask my mother because she would be very suspicious, and I can't go to a doctor without my mother finding out.
Petrified

It's true you have a chance, but not necessarily a good one. A woman gets pregnant while she is ovulating, which means producing an egg. Ovulation usually occurs around fourteen days before a menstrual period. You might get pregnant on that day, or the day before or the day after. But this varies such a lot that ovulation can occur anytime, even during menstruation. So you certainly are not safe.

The most reliable symptom of pregnancy is missing a period. Here again, however, confusion rules. Some women do have their periods while pregnant. Other symptoms are swelling of the breasts and morning sickness, which means nausea at any old hour of the day.

You can go to a doctor. If a reputable doctor agrees to see you, he will not inform your parents without your consent. He may refuse to treat you unless they know about it; this is his right. But once he has treated you, you are his patient, and it is unethical for him to tell on you. More likely he will try to help you tell your parents yourself.

The Planned Parenthood League performs pregnancy testing in some cities, for the low fee of three or four dollars. In other cities they will tell you where you can get it done.

Another good source of information is the student or underground press. Or you can call a laboratory direct (in the Yellow

Pages under LABORATORY, MEDICAL). They'll charge seven or eight dollars. Or your doctor can get it done for still more.

The test is done by a urinalysis, so you have to go and give the laboratory a specimen. You have to leave your name, but this is simply so they will know whose specimen it is. It takes from a few hours to a day. You call back and get the results. They don't tell anyone.

Contraception

Like every other thing connected with sex, contraception is a subject that is all muddied up with a host of other problems: myth, misunderstanding, religious beliefs, ethics, fear, and legal problems.

Parents are afraid that if they tell kids all about contraception, the children will be tempted to put this knowledge to work and become promiscuous. Kids are afraid to ask for the information, lest adults think they are considering being "bad," so they blunder into pregnancy unprepared.

There is really no sense in keeping kids in the dark about contraception, what to use and where to get it. There is a *lot* of sense in discussing when and where sex is a good idea, but this is a different question.

So here are the facts.

Withdrawal

This method of preventing pregnancy means the withdrawal of the penis from the vagina before ejaculation occurs. It can work all right, but it's not reliable. It requires king-sized self-control on the part of a boy when everything in his being is compelling him to go on to orgasm. When you realize that one orgasm is producing roughly 40,000,000,000 sperm, you can see how risky the method is.

Rhythm

This is the system advocated by the Catholic Church. It works better than withdrawal, but is still chancy. The idea is to avoid having intercourse during ovulation . . . but this is a gamble, because most women aren't perfectly regular. Most teen-agers aren't too good about keeping records, which is the only way you can find out if you *are* regular. And even if you do keep records and seem to be regular, you still can't be 100 per cent sure you are going to ovulate exactly fourteen days before each period. So rhythm is only somewhat better than nothing at all.

Condoms

These are thin rubber cases which are slipped over the penis just before intercourse. They are quite inexpensive and not hard to get. They are about 85 per cent safe, but fail if they leak or slip. Some men think they hamper sensation, but most find them satisfactory.

Diaphragm and jelly

The vaginal diaphragm is a dome-shaped rubber device which is filled with contraceptive jelly and then inserted into the vagina in such a way that it covers the cervix (the entrance to the uterus) and keeps the sperm from entering. It used to be the most popular method, and is about 90 per cent safe. One advantage is that it can be inserted well ahead of time. You do have to get one fitted by a doctor; cervixes come in different sizes, and the diaphragm won't work if it doesn't fit.

Many teen-agers fear doctors' appointments may embarrass or expose them. The expense is another disadvantage. Plus the fact that you have to remember to use the diaphragm each time.

IUD

The Intrauterine Contraceptive Device is a small coil of plastic, sort of like a pretzel, which is worn in the uterus. For some reason, when a foreign body is put in the uterus, it won't conceive.

The advantage of the IUD is that it only has to be installed once, so you don't have to remember anything. A small string hangs out to show you it's still there. It's about as safe as the diaphragm,

An IUD is seldom recommended for a teen-ager because it can be painful and unpleasant to insert, and cases of infection, while rare, have occurred, and threaten fertility.

The Pill

The famous Pill contains some male and female hormones, which one doctor described as making a girl "a little bit pregnant all the time." If your reproductive machinery thinks it has done the job already, it goes off duty. The great appeal of the Pill is that you don't have to fool around with any mechanical gadgets. Also, if used as directed, it is virtually 100 per cent foolproof. The disadvantage is that you *have* to use it exactly "as directed." It takes responsibility to remember to take your Pill every day twenty days a month and then skip it for ten. If you forget, you will be more likely to get pregnant than if you took nothing.

There have been lots of arguments about the safety of the Pill. The most worrisome side effect is the increase in blood clots it causes in some women, but this is extremely rare in adolescence. Less dangerous effects are swelling breasts, gain of weight (usually due to the body's retaining fluid), headache, and nausea. Millions of women feel the convenience and effectiveness of the Pill makes it worth the risk.

You should take the Pill only under a doctor's supervision. There are different kinds, and only he can help find the right one for you. Only he can give you the prescription, too. And you need follow-up exams once, or preferably twice, a year.

There are other methods kids try in emergencies, with varying degrees of success.

My girl and I went on a picnic and it was so beautiful that we finally did what we have been trying not to do for months. It was crazy, because we had no protection at all. Afterwards, she douched herself with a shook-up Coke. Would this have done any good?

B.D.

Not enough to rely on. The Coke bottle is rather a good shape, the carbonation helps the liquid to rise, and the slight acidity may do a little antiseptic work. But nature is against it. With all those sperm injected into the works, no douche can really be relied upon to get them all.

You need to remember that sex is a business with a serious result. There is a consequence to the act that has nothing to do with your immediate pleasures. If you feel mature enough to get into sex, you should be mature enough to treat it seriously. When you play Russian Roulette with pregnancy, it's not just *your* life you are involving.

You *are* pregnant

If you should find out that you are pregnant, the idea might be so overwhelming that you would not act at all at first. You might feel like this girl:

> *I'm sixteen and I'm sure I'm pregnant, and I'm so scared I just don't know what to do. I can't even do my schoolwork without getting a throb in my throat. I just feel like crying all the time. My mother tells me I must be in love, because I walk around the house in a daze.*
>
> *I told my boy friend, and he's really scared, too. He thinks I'll leave him, but I couldn't leave him and I know he wouldn't leave me. He does well in school and I wouldn't want to see him lose out on his future. He wants to go to college. He is a serious person. He's the oldest of eight children and has a lot of responsibility.*
>
> *I am respected among the kids because I don't go out and get drunk or smoke. I wouldn't want to lose this respect, but I don't want to get married especially.*
>
> *I want to convince my boy friend that it isn't all his fault. Is there a place I can call for help?*
>
> *P*

This letter shows just how terrifying pregnancy can be for a young, unmarried girl. It also shows many of the reasons why pregnancy is such a complicated problem. The letter writer understands very clearly that her life and her boy friend's may be severely limited by it.

Youth is supposed to be the time for kids to reach out and

discover the adult world and what their role in it is going to be. To be tied down to parenthood at this time stunts this kind of growth. You can't develop your resources. If you can't continue your education, you lose opportunities to test different kinds of interests and vocations. You lose the freedom to have fun, to try sports and art and theater, and to expand your social life. These things aren't just frivolities, either. They are the extras that make adult life rich and rewarding.

Pregnancy also has consequences for your parents, family, and friends. The idea of a daughter, sister, or even a friend being pregnant is a shock. It requires considerable effort to adjust to this.

And finally, there is the future of the unborn child to be most thoughtfully considered. To bring an unwanted baby into the world is the gravest sort of tragedy.

All this must be taken into consideration as you come to grips with the problem and try to figure out what course of action to take.

I am in terrible trouble and I don't know where to turn. I'm fourteen and I'm pregnant. My boy friend is sixteen and we have been going out for a year. We have been making out in his car but we were being very good until this spring. Then we just seemed to love each other more and more. And now this!

Where can I get help and how can I tell my mother? It will kill her.

Cora

No, it won't kill her. She will be shocked and angry and frightened, but then she will begin to help you.

What you fear first about being unmarried and pregnant is the shame. You are sure you will be condemned by everybody. It usually happens, though, that when there is real trouble, friends and neighbors rally to your support instead of scorning you.

It is not the time for passing moral judgments. It is the time to act, for unwanted pregnancy has such far-reaching effects on your future.

If you really can't bring yourself to tell your mother, then you should call an organization such as Planned Parenthood. These organizations all have trained people who have had lots of experience with your type of problem. They can help you tell your mother. Then they can help you and your family decide what is best to do.

I know it seems very frightening to make such a call, but all you have to say is, "Look, I'm a teen-ager in trouble." They will take it from there. Think of the relief it will be to get an experienced person helping you!

I am fifteen and will become a mother in seven months. My boy friend, who is twenty, asked me if I want to get married. He doesn't even have a job. I don't know what I should do. Please tell me, what?

Mother-to-Be

There are several things you can do. Marriage isn't the only solution.

You could have the baby. If you decide to do this you can stay at home and perhaps even go to school. Some high schools are now permitting pregnant students to continue. If your school does not, you may be able to go to a special school for pregnant girls.

Or you may want to go away. You could go stay with friends and relatives. Or you could go to a special maternity home for unmarried mothers.

If you have the baby and do not marry the father, you have to find out whether your family wants to keep it and can afford it. If not, you may decide to have it placed for adoption.

Or you may decide to have an abortion.

The right solution is the one that works best for you and for all the other people involved: the father, your family, relatives, friends, and the baby itself.

It is such a big decision that I strongly advise you to get help from someone with a lot of experience, a professional who knows what will work best in each individual case. Call one of the agencies that deal with these problems.

Abortion

I feel it is only logical that an unwanted pregnancy should be terminated and that those who want abortions should be allowed to have them. After a huge hassle over it, I finally had a miscarriage, so my problem is solved, but I feel sorry for others in my shoes. Why are abortions still illegal? No one who was opposed would have to have one, even if they were legalized.

Thwarted

Much of the opposition came from religious groups such as Catholics, Mormons, Greek Orthodox, and Orthodox Jews, who are all against it. Many Protestants are, too. They feel that life starts at the moment of conception, so taking the life of a fetus is murder.

Others believe that if abortion were too readily available, a casual attitude toward life and death would be created which would be wrong and against the natural instinct of preservation of the species.

Some people worry that it is unsafe medically, though it is quite clear by now that the reason for the dangers was that abortion was illegal and had to be done secretly.

Some black people fear that reform of the abortion laws could be a type of genocide for their race.

On the other hand, more people seem to be favoring the relaxation of the abortion laws these days. Like you, they believe that it is a mother's right to control the birth of her children. A surprising number of abortions are sought by married women who aren't ready to start a family, or feel they already have enough children to care for and support. Most abortions, though, are wanted by unmarried women, and many approve of this method to keep girls from being stymied by unwanted pregnancies.

Perhaps the most poignant factor is the fate of the unborn child. To be born unwanted and unloved causes some of the worst suffering a human being can endure. Psychiatrists say they see people who struggle painfully all their lives trying to make up for the love they missed as infants. Some people feel that until contraceptive measures wipe out accidental pregnancy (if ever), abortion is needed to prevent this tragedy.

To make abortion legal certainly would not force any reluctant woman to have the job done. Each woman must weigh all the issues before deciding what is right and wrong in her case.

She must consider what will give the least pain and the most relief to herself, the man, and their parents, and whether her pregnancy will bring forth a child who is truly wanted and loved.

Are there any physical dangers to having an abortion? Please don't tell me about the moral questions, as I have heard all those arguments. I just want to know what, if any, risks there are. My girl is scared.

J.V.

An abortion performed by a doctor under proper conditions has minimal risk. This is the same operation (called a D and C) that many women have because of various menstrual problems. There is some risk in any operation, but an abortion expertly done, and before the pregnancy is three months along, is remarkably safe.

But, an improperly performed abortion is something else, and very risky indeed. Abortion is actually legal in only a few states at this writing but most states are now liberalizing their laws, and in practice it is becoming much easier to get a therapeutic abortion. Still, you have to get a doctor's recommendation and usually the approval of a hospital committee. In some places it isn't automatic by any means.

Many abortions, therefore, are still performed illegally, and there are no standards that must be met. The operator may not be a doctor. The equipment may be inadequate and not sterilized. Infection is the greatest risk, and it leaves many women tragically sterile for life. Other dangers come from bungling the job or aborting women more than three months pregnant.

So you can see why your girl is scared. Have her call the

Pregnancy Counseling Service and get all the facts. If she really wants the abortion, they can arrange it. If she doesn't, you'd better stop trying to twist her arm.

> *Why are abortions so frightfully expensive? They are legal in my state but out of reach for many economically.*
> *Interested*

An expert abortion should cost about two hundred dollars. Doctors who charge four hundred dollars and five hundred dollars are simply making hay out of other people's problems. Not a pretty thing to do.

Because the neighboring states have laws against it, your state is having an abortion boom. If these other states relax their laws, the prices should come down. Meantime, there ought to be tighter state regulations. But don't be duped by the high price. Call the Pregnancy Counseling Service for a reputable and reasonable referral.

> *I'm trying to make up my mind about having an abortion. Are there usually a lot of psychological problems afterward? Do you feel really depressed? Also, how old do you have to be to have it done without your parents' consent in New York?*
> *Little Mother-to-be*

Psychiatrists say that there are normally no real psychological problems in women who have healthy psyches to begin with. You might feel a little depression, but nothing like the sense of loss you would feel if you had the baby, saw it, and then put it up for adoption. Then again, you might feel nothing but profound relief.

In New York you must be seventeen to sign yourself in.

You are very wise to be thinking this over so carefully. Only don't take too long. You can't wait more than twelve weeks from your last period to have a simple abortion.

To marry or not

I lived with a boy all last year at college and we were going to travel together this summer. When the time came, we decided it would be a good idea to take a break from each other and to look at our relationship with some perspective. So I came home instead. We may break up; I don't know yet, but I feel pretty bad about it.

Mother says bitterly, "What do you expect if you are just going to live with a man? Why don't you get married?" The way I look at it, it's lucky we weren't married. How can I convince her I'm not a "fallen woman"?

Constance

It will take time, for there are almost insurmountable differences in your points of view on this. For generations, people believed it irrefutable that sex was morally right only in marriage. Of course the rule was broken all the time, but this was always considered a sin — particularly so if a young girl was involved. It was a parent's bounden duty to keep daughters on the straight and narrow path to wedlock.

Even adults who aren't upset by the morality of premarital living together have strong doubts about its practicality. They worry that it brings great pain when such relationships split up, as you are finding out now.

This argument cuts both ways. If you and your boy friend had just been going steady, the break-up wouldn't give you so much grief. Living and sleeping with a boy makes your relationship more profound, so there are more bonds to cause pain when they break.

On the other hand, if you were married, the break might be even more painful. Divorce is a shattering experience, especially if there are children involved.

Many people consider unmarried arrangements like yours promiscuous. They say casual sex has become a fad. They worry that it will damage the concept of the family and that it will tempt little brothers and sisters into getting involved in heavy sexual activity much too soon. These are points worth considering.

There is evidence that the majority of couples who live together are not just casual or promiscuous, but seriously devoted to each other. Many are quite moralistic about their behavior. Many eventually marry. One factor that may be contributing to this style of life is that kids are now sexually mature at about eleven or twelve, but many are not finished with their educations until ten to fourteen years later. This is a long time to expect you to remain celibate.

The subject is controversial, to put it mildly. Some parents, like your mother, feel so strongly about it that when they find their own child living unmarried with another they feel that she or he is debased and has become almost a different person to them. Usually they get over this and realize it is the same old kid they always knew and loved. But it takes time — a long time.

Your answer to Constance sounds as if you approve of kids living together before marriage. My boy friend is urging us to do this and I want to very much, though I know it will shock my parents out of their minds. I'm twenty and he's twenty-one. Do you think we should?

Eve

I didn't intend to approve or disapprove. I meant only to present facts. One can't pretend the situation doesn't exist. It would be even more foolish to try to tell a person what they should do in this case.

To live with anyone, married or unmarried, you have to have a strong commitment to that person. Let's assume you love this boy very much. These are some questions you should be asking yourself:

Is he a man you could marry? If not, why move in with him? You may have some reasons: you may want to blow your parents' minds, or you may think it is a convenient, even chic and "with it" thing to do. But these aren't particularly good reasons.

If he is a man you'd like to marry, why don't you? There may be stumbling blocks: you're too young, not finished with your education, too poor, and not sure enough. If so, why don't you wait?

What will it do for your growth as a person? Your future life? Premarital sex undoubtedly runs counter to your upbringing. How guilty will you feel about that?

Keeping your baby

What do you think about teen-agers keeping their babies even though they aren't married?

Miss Lonelyhearts

Many more unmarried mothers have been keeping their babies in the last few years. Welfare payments have made this economically possible. Moral condemnation has lessened. Also, some girls have already left home and so have places of their own to take their babies to.

At first blush this seems like a wonderful thing. Babies ought to be with their mothers. Foster homes are not always ideal. Even adoption isn't 100 per cent satisfactory. A closer look reveals pitfalls.

There is no simple answer. The way to find what will work best in each individual case is to talk with someone trained and experienced in the field. Maternity homes have such people. So do many other social service agencies.

These are some of the questions they will want you to consider:

Where are you going to live? If at home, how does your family feel about it? Does your mother want the baby? If so, why? For your sake? The baby's sake? Or her own? Some mothers want to try to make amends for what they feel is their failure as a parent by taking care of the baby. It may cause contention later. You don't want fights over your baby.

How will you pay for the child? An allowance from your parents? Welfare? A job? If you decide to get a job, who will care for the baby while you work?

How about yourself? Can you finish your education? Your childhood? Can you complete your growth and be a mother at the same time?

And what about the child? What will its life be like without a father? Will it be as well loved as a bumptious two-and-a-half-year-old as it was as a cuddly three-month infant?

Why do you want to keep it? Some girls want to keep babies

out of social protest. It doesn't seem fair to the baby to use it as a weapon against society or parents. Some girls are just plain lonely and want a baby to love. Miss Lonelyhearts sounds like one of these. Babies need love, but young unmarried mothers need to take a long, hard look at their future.

*

The mere fact that contraception, pregnancy, and abortion are being written and talked about like this shows that there is indeed a sexual revolution. We have come a long way in a short time. But there isn't anything very new about this. Societies have always fluctuated between strictness and liberality in sexual behavior.

One big problem is that we are in transition. Older people don't agree with younger people. We do need to face the fact that conventional systems haven't worked perfectly. The present divorce rate is testimony to that. But it is too soon to tell how the new informal housekeeping arrangements will work. Perhaps most will end up in marriages and perhaps these marriages will last longer. They could hardly be much worse than many of today's marriages.

Some young people make this point. When you want to pilot a plane, you have to get your training first, and then they give you your pilot's license. At present, when you want to marry, you get your license first and then see whether you can make it work or not. It would be better, they argue, to issue marriage licenses to those couples who have already proven that they can successfully live together.

Whether households are communal or nuclear, married or unmarried, there is one person everyone has to be concerned about — the baby. There is nothing new about accidental children, but no perfect solution to their plight has yet been found. To my way of thinking, the only answer is to prevent accidental pregnancy in the first place.

10

Venereal Disease

Dear Beth,

My boy friend found out that he has gonorrhea and he's been getting the treatment. Now he keeps telling me I've got to go to the clinic, too, but there is absolutely *nothing wrong with me. Wouldn't I be able to tell if I were getting this disease?*

This chapter isn't going to make particularly pleasant reading, but V.D. isn't a nice subject. That's not the point. The only way to deal with an infection that is now pandemic in America is to learn what it's like and how to get it cured.

One of the reasons V.D. is so out of control is that 75 per cent of the girls who have gonorrhea show no symptoms. They're sure there is "*absolutely* nothing wrong," but there is. They've got the germs and are spreading them like wildfire.

Sex education in schools is helping somewhat. But there's still a long way to go or kids wouldn't be writing me letters like these.

What is V.D.? I mean, I know how you get it, but what kind of a sickness is it?

Just Curious

If you know how you get it, you know the disease is transmitted by the act of making love. Did you know that the name comes from the word "venery," which meant "pertaining to sexual love"?

The two kinds of venereal disease that are found most frequently (and I mean frequently!) are syphilis and gonorrhea. They are quite different except that they are both communicated in the same way, through sexual intercourse.

Syphilis is caused by a tiny corkscrew germ. Once it gets into the body, it burrows its way into the blood stream. Then it moves around through your whole system. The incubation period for syphilis is from three weeks to three months.

It may take years for syphilis to reach the final stages, but when it does, it can damage the hearing or the brain, and can blind and kill its victim.

Gonorrhea, which is more prevalent, is caused by a different germ. The infection stays more localized in the sex organs. It usually affects the urethra, which in males is the tube for carrying both urine and semen, or, in girls, the vagina and Fallopian tubes. It can cause sterility. The incubation period is from three to nine days.

A side effect of gonorrhea is that if a mother gives birth while she has the disease, her baby's eyes can be infected. That's why there is a law that drops must be put into all newborn babies' eyes.

Are the symptoms of gonorrhea the same as those of syphilis? Is it as dangerous?

Urgent

The symptoms are different. A boy first notices gonorrhea as a burning pain when he urinates. He may also see some yellow pus. This discharge will grow heavier if the disease isn't treated.

The scary thing about gonorrhea is that girls may have no symptoms at all. Some do, and their symptoms are like those of the boys. But many never feel a thing.

Gonorrhea is not as deadly as syphilis, but it is serious and can cause sterility. Girls can get "pus tubes," or scarring in their reproductive machinery, which prevents them from ever having babies. Arthritis is another complication, but rarer.

Can you please tell me the symptoms of syphilis? A friend of mine wants to know.

Andrew

Tell your friend the first sign is a sore, like a big pimple or cold sore (doctors call it a chancre). It usually appears on the penis (in the vagina, if your friend is a girl), but it could be on the mouth, finger, or rectum — anyplace where sexual contact is made. Sometimes it itches. Sometimes it is almost unnoticeable.

This sore will go away whether one gets treatment or not. This is the danger of syph. The germ is working away in there but nothing shows. Then in several weeks, perhaps six to eight, stage two appears. A rash of flat red spots, rather like measles, covers the body. There may be other sores. Hair may fall out in patches.

This stage clears up by itself, too, and the person wrongly assumes himself cured. Not so. In five, ten, even twenty or twenty-five years the ultimate damage may be discovered. The victim may become blind or deaf. He may have a heart attack and die. He may become insane.

If your friend suspects syphilis, urge diagnosis right now.

I can't think of anyone else I can talk to, but I'm afraid I may be going to get V.D. The only boy I ever went too far with has a bad reputation. Someone just told me they know he has "clap." Isn't this gonorrhea? What in heaven's name can I do now?

Petrified

Clap is a slang expression for gonorrhea. (So are "dose" and "morning drop.") Go to your doctor or a public health clinic and get tested right away.

This may sound impossible, but I am pretty sure I have a venereal disease. There are some physical signs. He's twenty-one but I'm only fifteen. I just don't know what to do. I'm afraid to tell my parents. If you advise me to go to a doctor, I'm afraid he will tell them. I just can't let them know, no matter what. Beth, I've got to have help!

Panicky

Doctors don't have to tell parents anymore in most states. Thirty states have changed their laws so that doctors can treat minors for V.D. without informing parents. Nearly all the rest are working to make these changes. And anyway, no reputable doctor would "treat and tell." Either he'd get your consent first, or he'd refuse to take you as a patient.

There are lots of other places where you can get help, such as walk-in clinics, the U.S. Public Health Clinics, or county health services. Look one up in the phone book or call any social service agency and ask for an address; they won't ask your name.

Treatment at public health clinics is usually free.

I have heard that if you take free treatment for venereal disease, they make you tell the name of the person who gave it to you. Isn't this "an invasion of privacy"?

Won't Rat

Think of it as an act of mercy. It is protecting innocent people from a very unpleasant disease. They don't make you, anyway; they beg.

V.D. is epidemic in this country. There are a million and a half cases a year. Six out of every ten people who have V.D. are under twenty-one. Eighty-five per cent of gonorrhea cases occur in persons between the ages of fifteen and twenty-nine. It can be cured so easily that there is no need for all this suffering. The reason for it is fear — fear of the shame of discovery — and this is largely groundless these days.

So for heaven's sake, cooperate with the authorities if they ask for names of infected persons. They aren't trying to pry or rat on you. The only way to stop the spread of V.D. is to track down everyone who has been intimate with those known to have it. You aren't doing anyone a favor by keeping their names to yourself.

I saw some pills advertised in the drugstore to cure gonorrhea. Are they any good? Is there anything you can take to cure yourself without going to a doctor?

Needs to Know

The pills may be some kind of antibiotic, but they won't be as effective as shots. You need a doctor to give these and to take the important tests to make sure the infection is licked. Don't be shy about going to the doctor or a clinic. It's the only way to get proper help.

If "off-the-counter" pills really worked, we wouldn't have this epidemic situation.

I'm a senior in high school and last year I had gonorrhea and was treated for it. The doctor said I was cured but now I have symptoms again. What went wrong?

Frank

You did. You were cured last year but have reinfected yourself. One of the many disadvantages of venereal disease is that you can get it again and again. The body does not develop an immunity as it does to most communicable diseases. So grab your girl friend and *both* of you go to the doctor.

A friend and I were arguing about this and can't find out the answer. Is it true that if you have intercourse a lot you will get a venereal disease?

E. McC. and G.B.

In one sense, no. The only way you can get infected is from a person who has the disease. So having repeated sex with a healthy person does not make you susceptible to V.D.

In another sense, yes. If you mean having sex with many different people, then your chances of running into someone who has it, and therefore getting it yourself, are much higher.

It is really not a question of how often, but with whom. Prostitutes run big risks of infection, but usually know how to take care of themselves. An ordinary person who is very casual about sex usually isn't so well prepared.

Is it possible to have both gonorrhea and syphilis at the same time?

G.W.

Yes.

Are there any other kinds of venereal disease besides gonorrhea and syphilis?

Just Asking

Yes, but they are quite rare. Chancroid, granuloma inguinale, and lymphogranuloma venereum are three of them, but unlike the two more common ones, they are local infections and do not spread to other organs of the body.

They produce sores, sometimes itching, on the sex organs. There is some swelling at times, and chancroid can be painful. They have to be treated medically as the other venereal diseases do.

*Isn't the rate of V.D. going up just because the popula-
tion is increasing?*

Philbrook

The rate of V.D. is going up faster than the birthrate. The
rise of venereal disease just has to be due to an increase of ex-
posure; that is, more people are having intercourse and passing
those germs around.

New sexual freedom among young people is part of the explanation. Here is one case where you really can take responsibility for some of society's ills.

V.D. has been around since history was recorded. No one
will try to blame you for starting it.

What counts is, who's going to stop it? The people who have
it. You might consider it as bad a form of pollution as that
which murks the air and waters. If you could start a campaign
to go get cured, you'd drop the statistics astronomically. You
could do it, too. No laws or establishment finks stand in your
way. And it would be a very sound accomplishment.

11

Depression

Dear Beth,

To look at me you would think I am the typical high school jock. I'm not too stupid in school and do pretty well at sports. I've got a girl and I don't hate my parents. But more and more lately I just can't stand myself. I look in the mirror and wonder, "Who is that fathead?"

My life seems meaningless. School seems boring to me, yet I do not have any idea what I want to do with my life. I get mad at people for no reason and feel bad afterward. Sometimes I just feel blah and I'm afraid I'm turning into a schizo. Is this normal?

Many of you feel blue and depressed about yourselves at times. When you are troubled by melancholy and a feeling of emptiness, you wonder if maybe you are sick.

Much of this is inevitable for teen-agers. You are in a time of transition. A little child has conflicts, but he doesn't question what he is. He knows he is a child. An adult has resolved the question, "Who am I?" and has the assurance of knowing where he fits in the adult world. But you are neither child nor adult, and it can be a very disconcerting feeling.

You are searching for what you want but don't know what this is. Sometimes you think you have found it but then it turns out not to fit after all.

Your life is new and your body is new. Your physical maturity pushes urgently for expression and won't let you forget.

See how your feelings can pull you two ways at once? Although you are thrilled by the newness, you are also apprehensive about it. You are excited by new tasks and goals but also long sometimes for the security of childhood days just past. You are fascinated by sex but feel shame at the same time. It is turmoil.

Your mood swings from feelings of failure, guilt, and not liking yourself to happy moments of excitement and well-being. This is part and parcel of your age. You need to assimilate your new feelings, your new yearning for human intimacy, new standards and goals, new rights and wrongs. This makes you introspective. At times this self-analysis is enjoyable. At other times it makes you miserable as all get out. This is depression. The question of how much depression is normal is difficult. In general, if you feel down now, especially if you have just had some rejection or disappointment, but still think that you are usually a stable person, your depressed mood is probably normal.

If you feel down and stay down, month after month without respite, if you don't seem to have friends or meaningful experiences, and if you have lost your sense of hope, then you would be wise to seek some help.

Anyone who has a worry that doesn't go away will always

find relief taking his or her problem to a trained professional counselor.

It may also help to read these letters from other teen-agers and see the kind of feelings they have been having.

The following letter is quite long, but worth reading, because it gives a remarkably complete picture of what teen-agers commonly feel depressed about.

I am so confused I just don't know what to do. This semester I have to decide what I want to major in. It must be really nice knowing what you want to do for the rest of your life.

I don't know what I want or where I am going. As a human being I often feel worthless, but other times I feel worthwhile.

I can't stand living going from one extreme to another.

Then I have to face the world problems. I just don't know who I can trust — Nixon or ?? At times I think our country is the greatest; then my mind will change.

Another problem is my generation conflicting with the other one. The older people think we don't know anything and vice versa.

The moral standards bewilder me. I have been taught that sex is sacred. Today it seems it is not. I used to think I knew the difference between right and wrong. Now I question myself.

Now the drug situation. I would like to get "stoned," but I would hate to take the consequences if I got busted. The temptation grows stronger every day.

As long as I can remember I have tried to talk to my father, but he just will not listen to me. The only time we

communicate is when we are fighting. We never accom-
plish anything except deeper separation. My Mom and I
can talk for a little while but she gets upset when I talk
about what bothers me.

Day by day I lose the desire of enjoying life. I used to
be a happy-go-lucky person. I don't feel like doing any-
thing. Help me!

Confused

Feeling confused is very unpleasant, but it shows you are
taking an active interest in the process of growing up. If you
weren't concerned about your future, but went gliding along
with the limited cares and interests of a child, you'd never make
it to maturity.

Being "concerned" brings worry and confusion and even
despair at times, but it is part of learning, part of sorting out.
Most teen-agers feel these black moods. When you think you
have found an answer, concern can also bring joy and elation.

When you worry about what to major in, you have a vast
picture of your future stretching ahead: who will you be and
where are you going? This is part of the identity crisis. A few
people have one overriding talent and seem blessed with the
knowledge of what their life will be — an artist, musician, or
scientist. We may envy them, though their lives can be narrow
ones. The rest of us have no such single force directing our
futures. We have to try out different things and discard many
to pick out what we want. You won't find where you are going
all at once. It takes years of testing and trying.

Your choice of a major doesn't confine you to one vocational
slot forever. You can expand, branch out, or even change directions completely. Don't deride yourself for being slow.

You're feeling worthless because you don't know who you are anymore or can't live up to lofty standards you have set yourself. As a child, you knew where you were going all right: "I'm six going on seven." Now you are searching and when you begin to find answers you will no longer put such a low value on yourself.

The ups and downs you feel are very common. It is partly physiological, perhaps, and partly because you are having to make so many decisions. You find the answer to one, feel good, only to have another pop up and "get you down."

When you outgrew childhood's world of firm rights and wrongs, you found adult human behavior more complicated than you'd expected it to be. The old rules are up for questioning. It is bewildering. Today, even some adults have doubts about some aspects of the old morality. More than ever you have to figure out just which answers are right for yourself.

Teen-agers have always faced temptations, and today drugs have been added to the list of forbidden fruits. You have the double job of making a moral decision about these things and then finding out if you have the will power to act on it. This is a tough test of maturity and judgment.

Fighting with parents is common. One can't grow up and away from them without conflict. You test your strength by testing your ties to them and this isn't always polite and cordial. Parents have reasons for fighting, too. They are often troubled by the problems their children face during adolescence. Maybe that's why your father won't listen, or your mother finds it hard to talk. They may be apprehensive themselves about the coming separation from you. They spent years of devotion raising you; they want you to have the best in life; so they fight to hold

on. And you may fight because you don't quite want to let go
yourself.

The thought of adult cares ahead is a pretty awesome thing.
No wonder you don't feel like doing anything sometimes. You
aren't sure what you are supposed to do, or if you are really
capable of doing it.

You aren't expected to be a mature, adult person all at once.
You have years yet to develop your opinions and choices and
values. School and college give you a refuge in which to work
without the full responsibility of adult life. Take your time.
And when you are taking stock, as in your letter to me, don't
neglect to give yourself credit for your good qualities and the
good strides you have already made.

> *I am fifteen. I get good grades and I know I'm not ugly,
> though a few pounds overweight. I get looked at by the
> girl-watchers, so I seem to be pretty normal. When I'm
> having fun, I don't think about things too much, but
> when I'm down, I get this strong feeling that there's noth-
> ing to live for.*
>
> *So many times I have told myself that I don't want to
> get old, and have to live all alone. So many times I've
> told myself I don't want to be around when the time comes
> for my mother and father to die. I don't think I'll be
> able to take it. I don't talk to them too much and some-
> times we fight, but deep down inside I really love them.*
>
> *JoAnn*

You are hung up because you see yourself in the future as if
you were still the young teen-ager you are today. You visualize

yourself as still being dependent on your parents, and wonder who will take care of you when they die. The fact is that you will no longer be helpless. You will have emerged from adolescence as an adult — a self-reliant person.

Young children have the illusion that their parents will live forever. When they learn about death, they assume that the next step after growing up is to die. Just like that. Naturally this makes them pretty reluctant to grow up! Then they learn this isn't the way life works. You have learned this intellectually, but some of the old fears take a while to disappear.

Think of it this way: You will have years, a whole generation quite possibly, to be friends with your parents, adult to adult, before they die.

There are times when I get really depressed and almost feel like committing suicide. One time I almost ran off from home, but I changed my mind when I remembered I had something to do for school which only I could do. Do you think I might be crazy? Or ought I to quit feeling sorry for myself and get to work?

Josette

All teen-agers have fears, and sometimes worry that they may crack up. Adolescence has dealt you a strong new set of impulses and basically you are afraid that you can't control them. As you grow you will become more confident that these won't get out of bounds. The fear that you may be going crazy will fade away.

It isn't a question of feeling sorry for yourself. A depression is a depression. Adults have them, too. But they have the advantage of knowing that blue moods are temporary, and next day they will feel better.

Teen-agers are apt to fear that when they lose self-esteem it's gone for good. This is such a depressing thought that they may contemplate suicide. Running away is another attempt to try to get away from depression.

Constructive action is a fine way to fight depression. Sometimes, though, when you have the blues, you feel so low you can't motivate yourself to do much. Volunteer work is a good idea for someone in your frame of mind, because you feel it is okay to work for someone else, even if you can't work for yourself.

The thing to remember is that moods do swing up again. Your view of yourself is low right now. It will bob up again soon.

*

Depression isn't just a teen-age problem. Everyone has days when they feel flat as a smelt. We Americans have a hard time accepting these feelings. We seem to think it is wrong or unnecessary ever to suffer. Got a headache? Take an aspirin. Feeling low? Try a drug.

There is some point to pain and unhappiness. If you sprain your ankle, pain prevents you from walking on it and injuring it further. If someone you love dies, grief helps you learn to live without that person. We have to bear such things.

One good result of teen-age depression is that you learn "how to take it." This will help you withstand the anxieties and buffetings that every person experiences during his lifetime.

12

Drugs

Dear Beth,
I have a problem and I don't know what to do. My boy friend is sixteen and I am fourteen and he is on heroin. I love him and don't want to hurt him, and that's why I can't tell his parents or the police. What shall I do?

Whose problem is it? Trying to place blame doesn't help much. Some people say you kids are lazy, undisciplined, and soft, and that's why you are turning to dope. Others say parents are too permissive, and that makes you the way you are. One parent even wrote me that this permissiveness is "because of Doctor Spock and all those other psychiatrists." Doctor Spock would be amazed to find he had started a cultural revolution!

Drugs are everybody's problem, and how we wish it would go away! Everyone who isn't directly connected with the drug scene is fed up with hearing about it. And maybe that's not all bad. People have been crying either, "Oh, the poor kids! Those tragically ruined lives," or, "Oh, those fiendish addicts! What sexual orgies and crimes." The first statement plays upon the emotions and the second overdramatizes. Both attitudes promote drug use rather than discourage it. Far better to defuse the interest in drugs by making true statements, such as "sad, dumb, boring, and wasteful."

The problem is severe, there is no question, but we need to put it into perspective. The answer lies in finding out who takes drugs, and what for. Of course, it is necessary to get help for the crises that arise, but this is like treating the symptoms of a disease. To find the cure we will have to discover what makes people need to use drugs in the first place.

We have learned quite a bit in the last few years. We have figured out that we are a nation of pill-takers, and most of us are habitual users of some kind of drug, whether caffeine, nicotine, alcohol, or tranquilizers. We know that Americans tend to reach for something for relief when we are under pressure, and that kids are under more pressure than past generations of teen-agers were. War, nuclear threat, population density, an intensely competitive society, and the fast pace of life press on us all — and you can't help but see how your parents look for solace in the medicine cabinet. But why do some kids go for hard drugs under stress, and other kids not? We are just starting to find out.

It takes a long time to reorganize the life-style of a country, though many of you are working at it. Meantime, the best defense against drugs is probably education. One chapter in one book won't add a great store of knowledge, but I'll try to answer the questions you ask me most often.

Legal drugs

Both caffeine and nicotine are drugs. They stimulate the body chemically. There are very few individuals in the country who never take a drink of tea, coffee, or Coke, so almost all Americans are getting fairly regular shots of caffeine. Is this a problem? No, because it is socially acceptable, and few people take enough to do themselves more harm than an occasional case of the jitters.

Cigarettes are another story. 'Tain't the drug that hurts you, directly, but the nicotine gives you enough of a kick to get you hooked. Then the other stuff in the smoke you inhale goes to work on your lungs and makes you susceptible to lung cancer and emphysema.

Why would anyone do anything as stupid as that? Because it is "cool." And then it's addicting. Probably most kids will eventually decide it is just too dumb to smoke. But teen-agers love to prove they are brave by living dangerously. So there are many of you who still smoke — along with your parents.

Don't you think a girl who is old enough to have her license is old enough to make up her own mind about smoking? If not, how old does she have to be?

Smoky

You always have to make these decisions for yourself. Even if you are forbidden to smoke, it is you who has to decide whether to obey, or to give in to the urgings of your friends.

The younger you are, though, the less equipped you are to make a wise decision. At fourteen or fifteen or eighteen, life stretches out endlessly before you. So what if smoking may subtract a year or two? The danger makes it all the more exciting. But when you get to middle age, you will regret having robbed yourself of any time at all. Try to imagine that.

Is it possible that at fifteen smoking delays the maturity of the body, or delays the menstrual period? Please give a definite answer.

Troubled

No.

My father has smoked for twenty years. Heavily. He tried to cut down a few times, but failed. I am worried about his health. How can I help him? Should I throw away his cigarettes?

G.W.

You can't quit for him. He has to want to do it himself, and after twenty years, he's pretty well addicted to the habit.

Throwing away his cigarettes will just make him sore at you. If you nag, he'll say you're an irritating child. Get some information from Smokers Anonymous; you can find them in your phone book. You can't join for him, but you could leave their pamphlets lying around, and this might plant an idea in his head.

Alcohol

Alcohol is the most widely used drug in the world. It is also one of the most dangerous. Yet we don't condemn it in this country, but encourage it. There are ads for liquor in all the media. Bars and taverns dot the roadsides. In many places, you are considered sort of an oddball if you refuse a drink.

Most states prohibit the sale of alcohol to minors, which in some states refers to people under twenty-one, in others under eighteen. But this doesn't prevent you from getting hold of it easily. Many of you learn the hard way how much booze you can take. Some never learn this.

In reasonable doses, alcohol can help some people as a "social lubricant." It relieves tension and makes them less shy. It quickly moves on to other effects, however, which the drinker is too numbed to notice. Inhibitions are released, and antisocial, boring, or aggressive behavior comes out. People can commit crimes while drunk. Coordination is affected, and accidents multiply. Addiction is real, prevalent, and dangerous, causing liver damage and eventual death. There are from five to nine million alcoholics in this country. It's a bad drug.

Alcohol acts as a depressant. People like to drink to forget their problems. It masks problems all right, but doesn't do anything to solve them. It creates new ones. We should all be a lot more cautious about the use of alcohol.

The trouble is that adults are used to alcohol. They aren't afraid of it, and they even expect their kids to "sow their wild oats" as older teen-agers. And you kids often find that drinking, like smoking, is the "in" thing to do.

In spite of the furor over other drugs, more kids get into trouble from booze every day than from pot, smack, or speed.

About two weeks ago my friends and I decided to go drinking. I had never thought of it before, but my friends convinced me that I should. I went, and got pretty well gone. Afterward I got into a heavy petting session with my boy friend, and now I'm scared to death I'm pregnant, I'm lost! I haven't told anyone.

Pam

Alcohol reduces inhibitions, so you lose your normal control over your behavior. You don't see, or don't care, what the consequences of what you do may be.

You may not be lost. If you skip a period, call the Pregnancy Counseling Service and arrange for a test, right away.

And if you decide to drink again, try to remember what amount of alcohol is a safe amount for you.

The other night my boy friend and his friends got drunk. The other girls all left when they saw the way the boys were. I think they took some other drugs, too, because most of them passed out fast.

I couldn't leave Jim in that condition. I walked him around until my legs ached. Then he threw up, and I was able to get him home. Did I do right? I was afraid if I left him he'd get in trouble, and I like him. How can I keep these kids from drinking again?

Junie

You did fine. It's a humane thing to do to stick by a friend in trouble.

Mixing other drugs with alcohol is real trouble. Booze intensifies the body's reaction to the drugs. Sleeping pills on top of liquor, for example, could put you to sleep permanently.

You can't stop others from drinking if they are determined to do it. If your boy friend continues, you can't stop him either. But you can refuse to go to those parties. Then he will have to choose between you and the drink, and isn't that the choice you want him to make?

Illegal drugs

Marijuana

*I am only in the seventh grade, and already many of my
acquaintances are smoking marijuana. There is only one
boy from my old school I can trust. I feel as though the
whole world is wrong. I can't sleep at night. My parents
don't seem to understand. I want to run away from everything.*

Iris

The only letters I get about marijuana are from very young
teen-agers who aren't familiar with it. For the older ones, it
has become so commonplace that one student said, "So many
kids have tried it that it's the ones who haven't turned on who
get the funny looks."

You often ask me why your parents are so upset. You don't
realize how new and strange grass is to a generation of people
who were taught that marijuana was for criminals, who never
bumped into it in the rest rooms at school, and who used the
expression "stoned" to refer to a guy who has had too many
beers. The Federal Bureau of Narcotics carried on a heavy
campaign against marijuana, saying it turned people into hard-
ened criminals and sex maniacs. This terrified parents. Such
scare tactics backfire and convince many kids that pot is an exciting and sensational experience they ought to try sometime.

The result of the campaign was the Marijuana Tax Act
of 1937. This made it illegal for anyone to have marijuana, and
thus prevented scientists from doing any research to find out
what the drug really does to people. Contradictory reports
appear every day.

Now parents are further scared because of the increase in the use of "hard" drugs. They are afraid smoking grass will get you into a group that uses other drugs.

And finally there is the very real danger that you will be arrested. No parent wants his child to have a police record. They feel you don't realize how bad this is. All in all, you can see why parents worry.

More research is now being permitted, and more people are smoking marijuana anyway, so we have learned quite a bit about it recently. Cannabis (the plant from which marijuana comes) is a mild mind-altering drug like alcohol. In small doses it makes you feel dreamy and good. The body does not build up a tolerance for it, so you do not have to increase the dose to get the effect. There is no physical addiction. There are no withdrawal symptoms. There is no hangover (though some kids dispute this).

There is still a lot we don't know. No physical damage has been found, yet. Marijuana is different from other drugs in that the chemistry of a marijuana "high" is not very well understood. It apparently affects that part of the brain which involves memory, and memory is still a rather mysterious function. It also interferes with the way a person receives or interprets the sensations he gets from the rest of the body — eyes, ears, and so on. This is the altering process. Sounds seem different. You see things differently.

Whether it can lead to psychological dependency is not clear. And though most experts now suggest it doesn't lead to other drug taking, I find there is still much doubt about this, especially among drug users themselves. So what are your questions about pot?

I'm confused about whether or not marijuana is sup-
posed to affect your personality. I smoke a joint occasion-
ally, maybe one or two a week. Can you tell me (1) Will
it make me want to try something stronger? (2) Will it
make me lazy? (3) Does it ever give you a real bad trip,
mess you up a lot, like acid does?

M.Y.

I don't think smoking once or twice a week will have much
effect on you, if you don't get caught. Being arrested and convicted can have a very real effect. Don't kiss it off lightly.

(1) Most experts don't find proof that marijuana use in itself makes you want stronger drugs. But it does put you in contact with drug users. It sets up a roadway to other drugs, if you
want to take it. Kids who have a very hard time coping with
problems in their lives welcome the respite drugs bring from
their anxiety. They will gravitate to more powerful drugs to
get more relief. If you can be sure you are not a dependent personality, grass will probably not lead to anything else. The
problem is, how well does a teen-ager understand his own personality? It hasn't fully emerged yet.

(2) There is lots of opinion on both sides of the apathy question. Experts have told me that grass does not make a person
lazy. If you are depressed, you are apathetic, and unmotivated,
and therefore lethargic. You may smoke marijuana to give you
relief from the depression. But it is the depression that causes
the apathy — not the pot.

Other people who have spent time with kids who have drug
problems tell me that pot heads, smoking as much as three or
four joints every day, really do lose their energy and drive. If

they can be talked out of using marijuana for a while, this lethargy disappears.

The experts would answer that by saying their depression goes away first; that's what gives them the courage to get their heads together and knock off.

The answer to (2) is — not proven.

(3) Grass doesn't seem to make you psychotic (mentally sick) unless you already tend to be this way. If you are emotionally unstable and susceptible, it may bring on temporary symptoms that are like mental illness.

Marijuana doesn't seem to give users really freaky times like LSD. It can trigger the return trip if you have already had a bad LSD experience. What marijuana does is reinforce the way you were before you took it. If you were sad, it makes you sadder. If you were happy, it makes you delighted. If you were scared, you become panicky. Temporarily. So the set is all-important here.

Tell me straight. Is grass an aphrodisiac or not? Some of the kids who have tried it say it is. Some say it isn't. My boy friend wants me to try it with him, but I'm scared.

Needs to Know

All those kids are right. Those who had sex on their minds before they smoked found the experience of lovemaking enhanced. Those who were thinking of other things got no sexual stimulation.

Like alcohol, pot reduces your inhibitions. If you are shy of sex, your boy friend hopes it will make you more daring. If you are scared, though, smoking may make you terrified.

I think you would be wise to settle the sex problem in your head while you are sober.

> *My boy friend was picked up for possession of marijuana. He panicked and tried to run away, and they were . . pretty tough on him. No one in his family knew where he was for a whole day. By the time they finally let him call, he had already said a lot of things that may get him into more trouble.*
>
> *Isn't anyone, even a teen-ager, supposed to be able to make a phone call? What else should a person do to help himself? Lots of kids are finding themselves in this predicament, and they ought to know what they are supposed to do.*
>
> Friend Indeed

Everyone is entitled to make one phone call when arrested, and it is the first thing they should ask to do when taken to a police station. A teen-ager should telephone his parents. If he can't reach them, he should call his most reliable friend, tell him exactly where he is, why he was arrested, and when and where he will be arraigned.

All persons who are arrested, including teen-agers, also have the right to hire a lawyer, and should get one immediately. If a teen-ager doesn't know one, or his family can't afford one, they should get in touch with the Legal Aid Society.

The arrested person should tell the police his name and address, but that is all he should say until he has talked to his lawyer. Officers will sometimes try to encourage him to talk. and a minor is especially afraid not to cooperate, but he can easily get into more hot water, as your friend did. He should agree if police wish to take his fingerprints, or search him. He should not try to talk his way out of jail.

*

Smoking grass seems to have about as much effect as drinking a couple of beers. Does this mean that it is safe for young teen-agers to use it? Not necessarily.

In the first place, it is illegal, and if you are convicted and have a record, it makes you a second-class citizen in many re-spects. Just using marijuana affects your thinking, even if you never get caught, because you're always being a fugitive. You may not consciously think about this, but the worry is always there. Some kids even get a kind of paranoia (fear that some-one is after them) when they are high.

A whole generation of kids is growing up with a disrespect for the law that isn't healthy for a free country. The law is a bad one, and is currently being reviewed. Penalties will be reduced, but legalization is more controversial.

The second reason why marijuana may not be safe for kids is that it sidetracks people from making decisions. Making choices is what adolescence is all about. What kind of people will you hang with? What do you think of your parents' way of life? A tough exam is coming up; will you study, or skip? Your parents don't like your girl; will you sneak out with her, or go along with their ideas? You have to be making tough choices all the time, and their significance brings you pain.

When you are high, little things seem important, and im-portant things seem trivial. You may concentrate on a tune or a matchbook, and let some big decision just drift by. For-get an appointment. Not take a test.

Smoking grass relieves you of pain. The more you smoke,

the more you can escape. Some adults feel this temporary kind of relief is not harmful. Many others are afraid it distracts you seriously from your main job — growing up.

You have to draw two conclusions about marijuana, depending on whether it is legalized or not. If it were, it seems on the basis of present knowledge to be less harmful than cigarettes or alcohol to people who have strong psyches. If you don't have a strong, self-confident, independent personality you would be better off leaving the stuff alone.

And how many teen-agers really know what their personality is like?

While marijuana is still illegal, it is dangerous for anyone to be involved with it. Kids who feel strongly about the legalization of marijuana might get to work to try to effect changes in the law.

The so-called "hard drugs"

I dated a boy for over a year, and learned to love him very much. But all the time I was dating him he was on drugs. It used to be just every so often. I could never count on him to pick me up on time, or even come at all. Beth, I am no longer dating him because now he's hooked something wicked.

I wish there was something I could do for him, but he acts like we're perfect strangers. What can I do to get him off those things I know are destroying him?

Hooked on Love

How does a drug "hook" you, anyway? Drugs are chemicals that affect your central nervous system — the regulatory agency in your body. They either speed it up or slow it down. Your body has a fantastic ability to try to keep itself in balance. It fights hard to compensate for what the drug is doing, and speeds up or slows down in return. If you take the drug repeatedly, your body gets into the habit of making the readjustment, and does it all the time. You have developed a tolerance for that chemical. Then you have to take more of it to feel the effect — to get high. You're hooked.

Stimulants

The drugs that speed up your body functions are called "uppers" quite often. The main ones are cocaine, amphetamines, hallucinogens, and also caffeine and nicotine. Cocaine is expensive and hard to get hold of, so I'll skip that and go on to:

Amphetamines

This group of drugs got into public use by prescription, to help people lose weight, to help truck drivers stay awake, and to help people like astronauts whose jobs call for a high level of alertness. Benzedrine, Dexedrine, and Methedrine temporarily increase mental activity, which relieves depression. People who find their world dull, monotonous, and hopeless are apt to turn to uppers for the euphoric effect of the high.

Along with mental stimulation, stimulants increase muscle tone and stimulate the heart and the whole central nervous system. The greatest danger is from an overdose. Toxic effects are anxiety, confusion, headache, and cramps. Extreme overdosage produces coma and death.

Why is speed so dangerous? A friend of mine has tried it a few times, and nothing bad has happened to him.

Billy

Methedrine has special dangers, one of them being that it is usually mainlined. Using needles makes you susceptible to dangers from infection and hepatitis.

Another danger is that speed, while not especially addictive physically, is highly tolerated by your body. You have to take larger and larger amounts to get the wanted high. This means the rest of your machinery is running too fast. Chronic use leads to exhaustion and collapse.

Large doses of speed produce paranoia, delusions, and hallucinations — effects similar to those of a serious mental disease. These are likely to make you irrational and very scared and possibly even violent.

What is a "meth crash" I keep hearing about?

Wonders

It is how you feel after a speed high wears off. Coming down from any high produced by a stimulant can be very depressing. Your body has been trying to slow you down to counteract the pepping-up effect of the drug, and when you stop the drug, the slowdown continues for a while. This makes you depressed. After a long period of use, the feeling of depression and exhaustion is so extreme it's called a crash.

My boy friend is a speed freak. Before it wasn't so bad. At first he was only smoking pot, but now he's using speed all the time. To support his habit, he pushes everything from grass to acid. What's worse, he's selling to my friends.

I tried to stop him. He says if I ever leave him, he'll kill himself. He's very serious, too. I want him to get help, but he won't. He's very sick. What can I do?

Despair

Unfortunately, the best intentions in the world can't do much to help people who are having problems with drugs. Sympathy isn't needed; they already feel sorry for themselves, or they wouldn't do drugs. And you can't usually talk them out of it. Your friend's threat of suicide puts you in a terrible position.

Go to see someone in your nearest drug center or walk-in clinic. This is too much for you to handle alone.

Hallucinogens

Turning on with these drugs has been well publicized for the psychedelic effects you get, such as seeing and hearing things in a new way, or seeing things that aren't there, or not seeing things that are there. Hallucinogens are also stimulants. Though they are nonaddictive physically, they can be habit-forming.

LSD, mescaline, and psilocybin are the three best known. The last two can be found naturally, but all three are most often chemically produced. Because they are illegal, there is no regulation, so you have no idea what you are really getting, or how much. Acid is so potent that an incredibly small amount is needed to give you a high. Three common brands are "orange sunshine," "purple double domes," and "white micro dots." LSD can be dropped on blotting paper (blotter acid) to be soaked off later for the desired effect.

Has anyone really died from taking acid, or is this just more propaganda put out to scare people off?

T.G.

People have certainly died after taking LSD. In some cases, that may not be what they actually took. A guy will assure you, "This is great stuff. Dynamite. Won't burn you!" But you don't know — *he* doesn't know — what it really is.

Other deaths from LSD are not due to its physical effects, but to the fact that it stimulates the imagination. Any teen-ager is apt to be worried and tense. Hallucinogens turn worry to panic. Users have run in front of cars, stepped out of windows, or drowned in rivers that they thought they could walk across.

I have heard many kids talk about LSD and how it really got their thinking together about life. They say they feel much better about themselves and were happier after taking it. Can this be true? And if so, how does it work?

Pat

LSD makes you overly sensitive. It stimulates your emotions, so what seemed like a good idea before you took it seems like a profound realization while you are high. The most common insight is that our life-style today is meaningless and people are just playing roles, not living meaningful lives.

There is some truth in this idea, all right, but LSD enlightenment doesn't provide permanent answers.

Depressants

People who are not looking for excitement, but find the world too painful to bear, turn off with "downers." Two kinds of depressants are barbiturates and narcotics — which include heroin.

Barbiturates

Barbiturates are used medically as a sedative and to control epilepsy. All barbiturates are made from barbituric acid, in combination with other chemicals, and they are put in pills or capsules. The trade names of some of the more common ones are: Nebutal, a solid yellow capsule, called a Yellow Jacket; Seconal, a solid red capsule, the Red Devil; Amytal, a solid blue capsule; Tuinal, a red and blue capsule; Luminal, which comes in pink, white, and green tablets.

The sedative effect of these drugs makes your personal problems seem to disappear. Side effects are mental confusion, inability to think, slurred speech, and drowsiness. Coordination and reaction time become way off, so driving while taking barbiturates is extremely dangerous.

They are dangerous in other ways. Tolerance develops very quickly, and you get a definite physical dependence on barbiturates. To fight their numbing influence, the body pushes back, stimulating itself. Therefore, when you stop the drug, withdrawal symptoms are hyperactivity, such as muscle twitching, and nausea. Violent withdrawal may produce harmful convulsions and delirium.

These sedatives are among the most dangerous of drugs. Misuse causes thousands of avoidable accidents every year — and 3500 deaths.

Narcotics

A group of drugs made from the opium poppy, and therefore called, sensibly enough, opiates or narcotics, includes opium, morphine, codeine, and heroin. Opium has been used since prehistoric times, and not long ago was the active ingredient in patent medicine. Those nice old bottles now selling like hot cakes in antique stores used to contain various "elixirs" that made your nice little old ancestors unwitting opium addicts. The Narcotics Act of 1914 put a stop to this.

Morphine is an extremely effective pain-killer, and also extremely addictive. It was used medically and it worked well, producing euphoria and freedom from fear as well as relief from pain. But harmful side effects come with it, such as nausea, vomiting, and constipation. Overdoses kill by causing respiratory failure.

Heroin

This is the most widely feared narcotic because it is so dangerous and so addictive. Actually, it was invented in a humane attempt to find a substitute for morphine that wouldn't be addicting. The name was to suggest that it was a heroic drug, but alas, its king-sized qualities turned out to be for evil, not for good. Heroin is more addictive than morphine, both mentally, because it so successfully masks distress, and physically, because the body adjusts to it so rapidly. Withdrawal is so unpleasant that it tends to encourage a user to continue on heroin in order to avoid the unpleasant experience.

Heroin is made synthetically, in illegal laboratories for the most part. It depresses almost all the body functions. Too much of it slows you down to death.

You can sniff heroin, or inject it into the skin (called skin popping), or into the blood stream (called mainlining). The use of hypodermic needles brings the added dangers of infection, hepatitis, and collapsed veins.

The first feeling you get from heroin is a warm, blushing sensation all over — the rush. After this comes relaxation and drowsiness. You are turned off, and out of it. There is no aggression or sexual excitement. The criminal aspect of heroin is real, but has nothing to do with the direct effect the drug has on the body. It comes later on, when the user wants to get more.

Is heroin really so dangerous? And if so, why do so many kids use it? And can it get you addicted against your will?
Worried About Friends

Heroin *is* so dangerous, because you have to build up such enormous doses to keep getting high on it, and an overdose of heroin — unlike some other drugs — can really kill you.

Kids who do dope do it because they feel the danger is less important than the protection the drug gives them from their mental anguish about their lives. People who work with drug users find that kids who become heroin addicts have four things in common.

(1) They lack self-confidence. These kids feel they are losers. They can't cope with life, so they want out.

(2) They feel very angry at their parents. They don't think they got as much love or attention or backing as other kids.

They may even be bitter that their parents didn't stop them from starting on drugs. They know heroin will drive their parents up the wall.

(3) They *want* to hurt themselves. People have a strange quality of turning on themselves when angry or frustrated. They feel so bad they don't mind if they are killing themselves. They may feel, "They will be sorry when I'm gone." Heroin is slow suicide, but meantime, it is dulling their pain, so they don't have to think about it.

(4) They are very dependent. In spite of the fact that they may hate their parents, 70 per cent or so of all heroin addicts live at home. They are down, depressed, full of self-pity, and can't think of any other way to help themselves.

As for getting addicted against your will, I suppose it is theoretically possible, but it isn't likely to happen in real life if you have a good "will." If you are not an addictive personality, and don't have the four qualities just mentioned, you could take quite a few doses of heroin without developing a need for it. So I don't think you need to worry about having it "slipped" to you unless you are craving some drug already.

Pushers don't create addicts. People who need dope go looking for it.

Why is kicking a heroin habit so hard? What happens to you? And can you die from kicking it cold turkey?

Will

Since heroin is one of the most powerful of the depressants, the body builds up strong defenses against it. That means it is going to be hard for the system to calm itself down after working itself up in a long battle with the drug.

The first step of withdrawal is similar to the flu, with chills, shakes, and a runny nose.

The second stage is a restless sleep.

Then comes stage three, which is the worst, and the one addicts fear. All the flu-like symptoms get worse, plus muscle spasms and kicking (hence the word you use for stopping heroin use). You get cramps and diarrhea and gooseflesh (the cold turkey). Even more painful is the mental distress of the return of all the problems the addict has been trying to avoid. This stage comes on two or three days after the last fix, lasts a day or so, and then tapers off for about ten more days.

It is not fatal.

Nobody writes me about crime, but it is part of the drug picture. This is the added ingredient that makes heroin use such a nightmare. To support a severe habit, a junkie has to scrape up from fifty to a hundred dollars a day. First he borrows, then he sells his parents' furniture, then he steals, becomes a pusher, and often a pimp. Once again, this makes drugs everybody's problem.

Heroin addiction is not hopeless. Many addicts are able to break the habit. No sure cure has been found, but what seems to help is finding someone who can build up the addict's self-esteem, through support and understanding, love if you will. This is what psychiatry and group therapy try to do.

Feeling sorry for an addict or coddling him doesn't help a bit. It is hard for parents to admit that a child is a junkie. But pretending he's not doesn't help him either.

But it is really not a hopeful picture. Many addicts don't make it. They either die of an overdose, or from hepatitis, or some other disease which can so easily attack their worn-out body. It is suicide, really, and very, very sad.

*

Some people feel that hard drug use is beginning to taper off. It is certain that many kids are beginning to see for themselves the real harm that heavy drugs can do. You used to pooh-pooh all adult warnings because many of the threats about marijuana proved to be exaggerated. But when you have seen addicts on the streets, or read of the death of Janis Joplin or Jimmy Hendrix, you know this isn't guff.

How do kids get into drugs, anyway? If you are a young teen, your first brush with dope is probably when you get into a group that is doing grass or acid. You buy the whole way of life of this group. One good way to direct your own behavior would be to take a look at this group, and see what kind of people you are getting with.

You may be somewhat ignorant about what stuff you are taking. Education in schools can be a tremendous help here. If you don't have that, go to a drug or youth center and ask. It is very important for you to know what various drugs are, what they look like, and what they can do to you. You really don't want to just grab and swallow anything that comes your way.

Look down the road, and see where a course of action like doing drugs will lead you. See where it has led others. Ask why you are doing it. If a friend is asking you to do drugs, ask him why *he* is doing it.

Short-term solutions for drug problems are getting better, though still far from ideal. Drug treatment centers are being set up all over the country. Some of them aren't very effective yet, but we are learning.

13

Too Permissive?

The methods parents use to get their teen-agers to do things, or not to do them, receive a lot of criticism from their kids. The kids usually feel their parents are too strict. But parents aren't at all sure of this. They are constantly accused of being too permissive.

Mothers and fathers have to set up certain restrictions. Kids have to shake the bars and yell, "Unfair!" at the tops of their voices. Part of the adolescent game is to keep pushing for more freedom. But kids don't really want the bars to disappear all at once. It gives them a feeling of support to know that there are boundaries within which they can operate. The time is fast coming when they will have to make all their own decisions, but they aren't quite there yet.

From a teen-ager's point of view, parents have the easiest part of the job. They look so self-assured and confident as they lay down the law. They aren't — especially nowadays.

Trying to launch kids into today's fast-changing world is not easy. Parents have to prepare their kids for a new way of life that is very different from the one they knew in high school. Some parents react by tightening the rules, others by being more lenient. Which way is the most successful?

In the old days, society set firm rules of behavior to guide the way kids were to behave. Now these rules have loosened. Teen-agers have to control more of their own behavior. I feel that the way to help them do this is to give them practice in making decisions at an early age. Strict rules do not give them the chance to use their own discretion.

Is this "permissiveness"? It's not a matter of letting kids do anything they want. It's a matter of teaching self-control. Kids flounder if there are no rules, but they need scope to test things out for themselves and see if they work.

Parents can start them young, with simple, safe choices such as whether to wear a sweater or what kind of boots to buy. As kids get older, bigger responsibilities can be added.

Teen-agers have to make some awesome decisions these days, such as what to do about sex and drugs. Those who have learned how to set standards for themselves and be responsible for their own actions are better prepared to cope.

There's no such thing as the perfect parent, just as there is no model child. There is disagreement over money, chores, the use of the car, and especially over dating. These letters show strong feelings from both sides about:

Parental controls

My parents are protective beyond belief. I can't even cross the yard without a lecture on half a dozen things to look out for. I realize they do this because they love me, but I'm strangling. I'm fourteen and my parents still insist on kissing me good-night and, of all things, tucking me into bed! Don't you think a good-night kiss is enough?

Hates Tucking

Many kids of fourteen don't like strong demonstrations of affection from parents. It smacks too much of being babied. Parents feel hurt when they are rejected, but wise ones don't force the issue. They realize when certain things are outgrown and settle for more grown-up ways of doing them.

We don't let our daughter go down the street to visit her girl friend because this girl has older brothers who we don't feel are a good influence. I'm afraid something will "go on" while she is there.

Alma is very resentful of this and also because we don't like her to hang around the bowling alley. She says she doesn't hang around and that her girl friend's brothers pay no attention to her. She'll be sixteen in three months. What do you think?

Alma's Mom

If she has a nice girl friend and it's a respectable bowling alley, I think she's old enough to go.

Parents are understandably anxious to protect daughters from the attentions of boys they dislike or from shady characters at bowling alleys, but girls have to learn how to deal with these things. It seems to me that Alma would be on safe ground in either of the situations you describe.

Punishment

My father always said if I did something wrong I should tell him and he wouldn't punish me for it. I broke something of his by accident. I did tell him and said I was sorry, but he yelled at me and said I have to pay for it. Do you think he is doing the right thing?

Sorry

If he made you stay home from the movies or something, you'd have a fair complaint. Paying for what you break isn't punishment; it's what all mature people do. Just being sorry isn't enough.

It's too bad he yelled, but that's something else you have to learn. It was *his* possession that got broken and so, naturally, he was upset.

I hit a baseball through our neighbors' window. They were away. I left money to pay for it but now Dad says I have to go over and apologize in person. I'm sorry about the window, but I just can't go over there.

Ben

Oh yes, you *can.*

My parents punish me by cutting off my allowance. Sometimes I don't have any spending money for weeks at a time. This is a pain. It's not that I'm really bad — I could understand it then — but I get docked for little things like having a messy room or being late to meals or missing the school bus. Last week I almost made it with-

*out any trouble, but then I dropped a milk bottle and it
broke on the kitchen floor. Half my allowance gone again.
Is this right?*

Penniless Pete

No, wrong. An allowance is to show kids how to make long-term plans with money. They have to be able to count on their allowance regularly.

The purpose of a punishment is to show a child what was wrong about something he did. The punishment must relate to the "crime." For instance, if your room is messy your belongings will get lost or broken. Your mother will have a hard time sweeping. The punishment should have something to do with putting away or sweeping so that you can see why these things are necessary.

If you miss the bus, you might be asked to get to school on your own, even walk. Being late for school makes teachers mad. You'll be rushed and not do your work so well. You learn, of necessity, that it's worthwhile getting to the bus on time.

Taking away your allowance has no bearing on these things.

*I'm fourteen and have no intentions of going out alone
with a boy. I just want to double date with my friends and
have some fun. Recently I was caught betraying my parents and I am being punished. I believe in punishment,
but this is too severe. They say I may not date for five more
years! I'll be nineteen! This overstrictness is bad because
it makes me feel like doing terrible things just for revenge.*

M of M

It's good you understand your parents' anger and alarm about your sneaking out on them. I suspect that this five-year ban is a cry of outrage and that they will soften up long before you are nineteen. To speed that process, do your penance gracefully and stick to the rules, which will show them you are responsible and able to handle more freedom.

If they don't let you off the hook, they will be unwise, for you are right in thinking that overly strict punishments bring about just the opposite of what parents want.

Invasions of privacy

One day I caught my parents both reading a letter to me from a pen pal. I was really upset. They said it was their privilege to read any of my mail until I am twenty-one. I regard my letters as personal. How can we teen-agers trust and confide in our parents if they don't show any trust in us?

Indignant

How indeed? I think this is an unfortunate line some parents take. As children grow into adolescence, they begin to have more of a private life and become more reticent about sharing all their thoughts with their parents. Sometimes parents then jump to the conclusion that their thoughts must be bad. To save you from yourself, they try to ferret out your secrets by any means, fair or foul.

This destroys your trust in them, as you say, and ruptures good communication. Parents want their kids to be honorable and reliable. But you only become trustworthy by being trusted. Spying and snooping forces you to become secretive. A parent may have the legal right to read his children's mail, but he accomplishes only harm by this violation of a child's privacy.

Chores

I have always thought that one of the biggest causes of teen-agers' unrest and antisocial behavior is the lack of a useful role for them in today's social setup. In the old days their help was vital to the running of the family. Now houses and offices don't need them. Gadgets do the housework. Jobs are so specialized that untrained youths can't help. It is great to have the kids do the dishes and mow the lawn, but this doesn't have the satis-fying importance of spinning wool for the family blankets or chopping wood for the family fire.

So what are parents to do? Kids should be depended on to do their fair share of the boring chores. But they need more than this. Kids can take on increasing responsibility for dif-ficult jobs and do more of the essential planning. Instead of just having Susie make the salad and set the table, she can take the week's money for food and do the budgeting, planning, and shopping. Sam can still wash the car, but he can also take over the job of seeing that it is regularly greased, that the oil is changed, the wheels rotated, and stuff like that. If he feels responsible for the car, he'll drive more carefully, too.

Teen-agers know when work is made up for them to do. They are almost adult in strength and ability and they want challenges to prove this maturity. In the days when a boy had to drive a plow, he showed the world he could do a man's work and he used up a lot of energy in the bargain. Now we have to provide substitutes. Some kids find their challenge in sports. Some lucky few get to go to camp or take part in Outward Bound experiences that really test their mettle. Those who have no such outlets may try to provide their own testing grounds in the city by stealing cars, drag racing, or shoplifting.

Teen-agers can and should shoulder some of the real and necessary family jobs. They will rise to the opportunity and be eager to show how capable they are. They may surprise parents with some innovative and practical systems, too.

I don't know how much time to ask my teen-aged children to spend working on weekends. We expect them to help with the lawn, the car, and some housework, but there is constant confusion and conflict with their social life and homework. We try to set a fixed time, but there are always excuses, and often my husband and I have to finish the work ourselves. What is a good way to arrange chores?

Mrs. Blank

Let the kids be accountable for when they do the work. You might have a family policy meeting and decide who can best do what jobs. Divide up the boring ones that nobody likes to do. Get your children's agreement on what their chores are to be, and when they have to have them completed — probably before Sunday evening. Leave the rest up to them. This won't produce perfection, but it should cut down on the conflict.

My parents make me baby-sit for my younger sisters every Saturday night. They say it is their only night out and it's my duty as the oldest to help out. This just about wrecks my social life. Aren't I entitled to a Saturday night date of my own?

Bill

Seems so to me. Saturday is a popular night for teen-agers, too. Can't your parents afford a baby sitter? Perhaps you can suggest one of your friends who happens to be dateless. Surely a compromise on alternate Saturday nights could be worked out.

Our high school daughter has always been cheerful about helping around the house. Now she is still cheerful, but never has any time to do anything. She has more home-work, I realize, and more school activities, clubs, and social life, so she never gets around to the jobs she says she will do. Should I let her cop out, or what?

Mrs. V.

Teen-agers need to invest in themselves. Parents want this experience for them and may wisely relieve that child of some of the time and energy that formerly went into helping the family.

If your daughter is doing things that contribute to her growth and education, this may be more important to her future than doing the chores. If you don't really need her help, you can, in good conscience, let her do less work.

If you have any other children, be sure to make this very clear to them or they will feel it is grossly unfair.

I don't mind doing chores for my family, but I wish my parents would decide ahead what they want me to do and stick to it. Especially on weekends. Usually, just as I think I have all my jobs done and start to go off with my friends, it is, "Oh, Rick, will you please wash the car? And while you're at it, fix the garage door." This wrecks my plans.

Rick

This is a reasonable gripe. Can't you ask your parents to give you either a set list of jobs before the weekend or a set length of time they desire you to work? You will have to expect a few exceptions under special circumstances, but this should make planning easier for you.

Money

This is a subject that spoils friendship, ruins marriages, and does little to smooth relationships between parents and teen-agers. Parents have the dough, the kids need it, and parents are supposed to provide until children are old enough to earn their own. Too often money is used as a whip or a bribe, a threat or a reward, when it really is just a means to an end.

Parents who want their kids to learn the value of money should teach it to them. They shouldn't invest it with an emotional value it doesn't have, but they need to show their kids that all adults have to be able to come up with enough of the stuff to feed, clothe, house, and entertain their families. So they try to teach their children how to earn money and save it, budget, lend, and spend it, too.

I am truly puzzled about how much money to give my fourteen-year-old daughter. She wants to buy her own clothes, and I agree. What do most parents give their children for a clothes allowance?

Teen's Parent

It is impossible to give an exact figure because there are so many variables — family income, the cost of living in your area, how clothes-conscious your child is, the standards of her school-mates, and so forth.

Try to figure out how much you spent on your daughter last year. Average it out on a monthly basis. Add enough for movies, carfare, lunches, and whatever else she will be liable for, and start out with that amount. No law says you can't revise it up or down later.

It may seem like a large figure. Perhaps you will start on smaller amounts, with you buying expensive items like coats. To give too little doesn't teach how to budget, because kids are constantly thwarted. To give too much is bad, too, because then they become careless.

If your daughter makes many demands for advances, check to see what she is spending and if you have given her enough. If so, let her earn the extra. But don't interfere with the way she spends unless she asks for advice. She needs to learn how to shop, too.

My dad will never give me any allowance in advance. Do you think it is wrong to loan your teen-agers money?

Ned

Loans are necessary on occasion, but on the whole, it is better for parents to encourage you to save up ahead. In adult life, when you take out loans you have to pay interest on them, so it's an expensive habit.

The car

What do you think about a boy of seventeen getting to use the family car? My mother and father each have a car but they will not let me use one for dates because they say:

(1) The cars are theirs.

(2) I am too young to use a car on a date.

(3) My marks aren't good enough.

I pay the extra insurance required for drivers under twenty-five. I offered to pay something from the money I earned last summer to help pay the expense of the car. I would pay for my own gas and keep the car clean. I only want to use the car one day a week for a date, a total of about five hours. Is this asking too much?

Reluctant Bus Rider

No, it's not. Most boys of seventeen have this privilege, and not all of them pay for their own insurance or contribute to the cost of the car — though I think this is a fair arrangement. A boy should certainly pay for his own gas.

Of course your parents have first claim to their own cars, and they may even object to your reserving one for a special time each week. However, when they aren't using both, it seems only fair to lend you one, with three big ifs:

— If you need it for transportation and not just to show off your new position as Licensed Man.

— If you have proved you are mature enough by fulfilling your responsibilities in general at home and at school.

— If you know the rules of driving, including the legalities involved.

Your parents' reasons are really not logical:

(1) They own the house, too, but they let you share that.

(2) The state considers you old enough, or wouldn't have given you a license.

(3) Marks have nothing whatever to do with driving ability.

I am eighteen and I've been saving up for five years to buy a car. Now that I've got enough money, my mother is having a fit. She says it's kids like me who cause most of the accidents, that my work will suffer, and that I'll want to show off and drive like a fool. My father is behind me and says I'm a good driver. How can we calm down Mom?

Abe

Your mother is right about the accident rate. Boys under twenty have the highest accident rate. Kids of twenty to twenty-five have the highest rate of serious accidents. Her worries have basis in fact.

However, your father's confidence in your driving ability should carry a lot of weight. If you are stable and responsible (and earning all that money is a pretty good sign that you are) you will probably take extra good care not to crack up a car you have earned yourself.

Social life

Teen-agers are under a lot of pressure from their friends to be free, to go where and when they please. They transfer this pressure to their parents. This makes for a lot of disagreement.

Adolescents are still young enough to need the protection

of fair rules and the support of reasonable limits. If the ground rules match the social patterns of the neighborhood, and if they are set up with teen-agers' happiness in mind as well as their safety, then kids will probably go along with them, grudgingly. But these kids are old enough to be having a pretty active social life; there needs to be a little stretch to what's fair and reasonable.

Tricky problems come up over boy and girl friends. Suppose parents don't like them. Suppose they downright disapprove. Parents are always worried that their kids will fall into "bad company." All through life we meet people who are potentially a bad influence. To have the sense to recognize them as such and to resist their inducements, we have to have had some negative experience. So overprotection can be a mistake. Merely palling around with nice kids doesn't give a teen-ager much to go on.

This doesn't mean you want to introduce your children to juvenile delinquents, but I think parents will do well to give their teen-agers increasing responsibility in choosing their own dates. Kids get a realistic view of the world by meeting others of different religions, backgrounds, temperaments, education, race, ability, and so forth. Then these teen-agers can see for themselves what kind of relationship works best for them. My hat is off to parents who have built a foundation of self-respect, high standards, and responsibility in their children so they can trust their judgment in picking dates. These kids will find the assets and liabilities in different boys and girls, which will do them a big service in the business of growing up.

It is a big problem to both teen-agers and parents, so I get loads of letters on the subject. Like these:

I want to stay out with the rest of my friends after school but my mother won't let me. She says I have to be in by dark every night and it's dark by 4:30 P.M. these days. She is always after me to make friends and do sports and things with the other kids, but how can I if she keeps me in like this? I am thirteen and old enough not to be treated like a baby. Isn't she old-fashioned?

Baby

She's sensible. The kind of sport you play after dark is called "hanging around looking for excitement." This isn't the kind of sport your mother had in mind.

My husband teases our boy because he doesn't date any girls yet. He's a big, strapping fifteen-year-old and perfectly healthy in every way, but seems to be a slow starter with girls. His father feels it is a good idea to try to josh him out of this and keep him from taking himself too seriously, but the boy hates his father's joking about him, and cringes when he does it.

Mrs. Jacobs

Teasing doesn't accomplish anything except humiliation. It is unwise to pressure kids about dating. I'm sure the boy's father hopes to build his son up but if he could feel how unsure teen-age boys are anyway, he'd realize that teasing is just hitting the guy when he's already down. If he is worried about the boy's "masculinity," he needn't fear. Most fifteen-year-old boys who show no interest in the opposite sex wind up happily married.

I'm a sophomore and used to go to school dances on Sunday nights from seven to ten. Now my parents won't let me go, because the dances are held on a "school night." But they let my brother play indoor tennis until eleven each Sunday night. The dances are regular, chaperoned affairs. I don't think it's fair!

Loves Dances

I don't either. I think it is bad timing on the school's part, but if they are regular dances, it really doesn't seem fair not to let you go.

Our daughter worries about being unpopular. She has only one good friend. She'd like to have boy friends, too, but at fourteen she isn't making much progress. Is there anything we can do to help her?

Marcie's Parents

You can help her general attitude by trying to build her self-confidence. Don't smother her in compliments, but show her in practical ways that you approve of her as a person, admire her abilities, and enjoy her company.

Our teen-agers are balking at our regulations about dating, so I thought I'd ask you if we are being too strict. We say no dates on school nights, and home at eleven other nights, if you are under sixteen. No friends in the house when parents are not at home. The last item is the present bone of contention. "All our friends" have parties when their parents aren't home, say our children. What do you think?

Mr. and Mrs. J.F.

I think your ground rules are about average for most high school kids. Stick to them. You can make exceptions for valid reasons, such as a school play on a school night, or a party that lasts until 12:30.

But don't weaken on the "No partying in a parentless house." Even the most innocent teen-agers can get overexuberant, to the detriment of rugs and furniture. And not so innocent teens can get into beds or get into pot, to the detriment of their welfare and their police records. Every day there are stories of raids on nice suburban homes. Young adolescents need chaperons — period.

Our high school junior is taking up with a boy who has a very shady reputation. He was convicted of car theft a year and a half ago and put on probation. Nancy claims he has gone straight, but he seems most unsavory to us and we forbade her to see him anymore. This caused such violent tears and recriminations that we were afraid Nancy might do something desperate. We told her we'd think it over.

Unsure Parents

A person who has made one mistake deserves another chance. You want to look at this boy for what he *is,* not just for what he did and was punished for. Car stealing is a bad business, but many otherwise honest boys get pushed into it once as a sort of "puberty rite." This doesn't condone it, but does mean these boys aren't heading for a life of crime.

If you reconsider, ask Nancy to bring her boy home so you can get to know him. If she is really nutty about him, you will want to find out about his family. Probably she is not serious, yet. Love does muddy up a girl's judgment, but have some faith in her good sense. The chances are that this won't be her permanent love, but violent objections on your part will tend to make her care more about him, not less.

Why do my parents have a fit every time I get asked for a date? I am seventeen and have been dating off and on for a year with different boys. My parents almost always let me go, but first of all there has to be an international conference about who the boy is and where we're going. Is this normal?

Elsie

As normal as ants at a picnic. Parents don't always handle things gracefully when their daughters first start dating. They want to give their girl enough freedom to have fun and get to know boys and eventually find a husband. But they also want to set proper limits for her safety. You can be glad that your parents are concerned enough to want to find out what you are doing and with whom, while at the same time they trust your judgment enough to let you go.

My daughter is going off to college, and I have been wondering whether or not I ought to get the Pill for her. I have read the statistics, and I know perfectly well that the pressure on girls to allow intercourse is very high. I hope my girl will wait for marriage, but even more, I hope she won't get pregnant. What should a parent do about this?

AZ

Ask your daughter if she knows how to get a prescription for the Pill should she ever decide she needs it.

Girls ought to handle this themselves so that they will have to make their own decision about sex. If parents dole out contraceptives, they seem to license their girls to proceed without having to take responsibility for their own behavior.

Most colleges have facilities for students to get contraceptive advice.

Our son Jay is a junior at college. He asked and received permission to live off campus this year. I thought he just wanted to get away from campus life and be more on his own. Was I dumb! I recently overheard one of his friends say, "Jay is living with his girl friend and another couple. What a set-up!"

I was staggered. I know these arrangements are becoming quite common, but I never dreamed one of my own kids would do it.

I just know it is wrong. No matter what kids say, they can't change the fact that promiscuity is immoral. How can Jay so lightly throw over twenty-one years of upbringing? I feel so angry I sometimes want to cut him out of the family. My wife says to wait and cool off. Jay really likes this girl. What can a father do?

Mr. R

What seems so fundamentally wrong to you is not a matter of fact but a matter of opinion. Many members of today's generation have decided that a legal marriage certificate isn't necessary to formalize their commitment to each other.

They do not feel they are being promiscuous. Most of the college-age kids who set up housekeeping together do care for each other, and most eventually get married. Some of these young people are acting out in defiance of the older generation, and are very casual about their sexual behavior, but most are actually quite monogamous, even prissy. They feel that the present idea of marriage, with quickie divorce and a high level of infidelity, is more immoral than their way of life.

Let Jay know you are aware of his living arrangement. It will be a relief; most kids hate acting behind their parents' backs.

Tell him exactly how you feel. Don't blow up — just state your opinion. You have indicated faith in his ability to run his own life by sending him off to college. You shouldn't try to control him now. But you are still his father and he is entitled to your wisdom, even if he doesn't act on it.

*

I think it is important for both kids and parents to look to the future and to try to conduct their campaigns with all the tact and understanding they can muster. Eventually, parents will find that their kids have grown into attractive adults. Surprisingly enough, kids will find just about the same thing. A story about a boy going off to boarding school is a good example. He left home a sophomore, disgusted with how naive his father was. Three years later he returned home and was terribly impressed to find how much his father had "matured."

There will always be the Pubic Wars. If both sides make a hearty effort not to inflict irreparable scars while you fight, you'll win through to a lasting affection and respect that will give you joy and comfort for the remainder of your life.

14

Will You Make It?

The problems you struggle with as teen-agers are the same problems you will be struggling with all your life, to some degree. You never outgrow the desire to relate to others, to have friends, to be confident, attractive, and happy. All your lives you will yearn to express yourselves well in friendly conversation, in serious discussion, in sex. If your adolescence worked out well for you, you will have tested yourself in many different situations and made a good start at handling these problems. You will know much about your abilities, your temperament, and how you fit into the world.

You are growing up in a very special time. A revolution in thinking is going on in this country. The activism of young people has been felt in major issues such as civil rights, war and peace, feminism, ecology, and the reshaping of traditional morals.

You are the television kids. An idea born on the West Coast yesterday is part of your thinking on the East Coast tomorrow.

Change has become the way of life, and growing up is more complicated than ever. So much is getting thrown at you. Get any group of adults together these days and sooner or later — sooner, probably — the talk gets around to "the kids." Some adults will roll their eyes and groan that "Young People aren't what they used to be." Sure you're not just the same. And you're not perfect. But the world isn't the same, either. Many of you have the determination to do something about this world and nudge it a little in healthier, cleaner, more peaceful, and more loving directions. I'm convinced that you will make it.

There are indeed things you can't ask your mother. But there are other things you can tell her. And she will learn something if she listens. I have.

DATE DUE

JUL 12 7?			
MAR 21 78			
OCT 18 ⌐3			
GAYLORD			PRINTED IN U.S.A